ELVIS FOREVER:

LOOKING BACK ON THE LEGACY OF THE KING

BOZE
HADLEIGH

For more information contact:

Riverdale Avenue Books
5676 Riverdale Avenue
Riverdale, NY 10471.

www.riverdaleavebooks.com

Design by www.formatting4U.com

Cover Art by Scott Carpenter

Digital ISBN: 9781626015951
Print ISBN: 9781626015968
Hardcover ISBN: 9781626016033
First Edition September 2021

Dedication:
To Ronnie

Table of Contents

INTRODUCTION

It's been said that his music is the background to our idealized lives. To this day, no one has outsold Elvis Presley. Initially a regional singer of country and "hillbilly" music, he broke through nationally with rock 'n roll, a youthful phenomenon deemed controversial and threatening to the establishment, as was Elvis himself. His voice and appeal enabled him to span all genres of music and move on to greater fame on the silver screen. Having been denounced as a shameless exhibitionist, for some time Elvis symbolized youthful rebellion and freedom of self-expression. Presley's life and times and music still resonate because he embodies so many strengths, weaknesses and contradictions of the tarnished American dream.

He rose from poverty to tremendous wealth. He spread some of it around, yet exacted an increasingly high price from those around him. Money initially brought pride and satisfaction but not lasting happiness. Originally a risk-taking trendsetter, Elvis became more and more a part of the establishment and fell into a creative rut after giving up in-person entertaining for the easier and better-paying career of a movie personality. From "too sexy" he became prudish, with sexual hang-ups unknown to the public till after his death. He projected swagger and self-confidence but had a lifelong fear of being laughed at and rejected, as he so often was in his youth.

But by his mid-30's he staged a second-act comeback that revived his career and interest in Elvis Presley as a cultural icon. Had he not experienced his dispiriting career low he couldn't have risen like a phoenix to new heights of popular performance and public appreciation.

It's been said there are three Elvises: the hip-swinging rock 'n roll Elvis, the bland Hollywood Elvis and the flamboyant Las Vegas Elvis. In effect there are as many Elvises as there are Elvis fans. He means different things to different people. Individuals take what they want or need from his legacy. He still entertains us, whether it's people listening to him sing, watching an Elvis "tribute artist" or even an Elvis Presley movie, touring Graceland, viewing an Elvis concert on DVD, talking about Elvis or reading about him—he's never boring. The unique first name that requires no surname to spark recognition and lively comment remains universally recognized and prompts everything from smiles, nostalgia, a sense of loss, enjoyment, desire, admiration and pity to continuing fascination and personal identification.

PART ONE:
GROWING UP ELVIS

Growing Up Elvis

Elvis was the survivor of twin boys, a fact that strongly influenced his life. Mother Gladys, fearful of losing her only child, kept him close. The mother-son bond intensified when father Vernon was away working, seeking work or in jail. Growing up and in school, Elvis was a loner, often shunned by classmates due to poverty, the way he dressed and his longer hair. As his parents' marriage deteriorated, Gladys's sole focus became her son, whose fondness for singing she encouraged. She steered him away from his interest in guns, which would later prevail, and helped young Elvis pay for his first guitar.

The Presley family was poor to the extent that Vern couldn't pay for the $3 marriage license, and public relief provided the $15 delivery fee for Elvis' birth. The trio was evicted from their home more than once and Gladys was mortified when they temporarily had to take welfare. At different times both parents worked or one did or both were unemployed. Eventually teenage Elvis took a job while in high school, but his grades suffered and he was falling asleep in class. His mother, at any rate, convinced him to stop working and remain in school. He became the first Presley to earn a diploma.

Initially Gladys was pleased with her boy's singing success. Until his career expanded to the extent that he was often or usually away from home and becoming involved with his (female) fans and strangers (business associates). The burgeoning publicity intimidated Gladys and media criticism of her too-sexy son embarrassed and angered her. Her fragile health worsened as she gained weight and developed a drinking habit. Elvis' stardom did not make her happy, and a primary reason he bought Graceland was to afford Gladys privacy—neighbors and strangers used to stare when she was outside and fans would steal articles of male clothing off her clothesline.

The death of Gladys Presley at 46 was the biggest tragedy in Elvis' life and impacted his health. Doctors had to prescribe pills, commencing a growing and eventually fatal habit. Additionally, Elvis developed a sexual hang-up whereby he was averse to sleeping with women who'd conceived (later including his own wife). For Elvis there were three types of females: virgins, bimbos and mamas.

"His parents were near-indigent, it wasn't a happy childhood, etc. But I don't feel too sorry for him because by 21—which was the midpoint of his life—he achieved fame, fortune and adulation such as few human beings ever do."

—Broadway star, **Patricia Morison**, who lived to 103

"He was a lonely boy. Lonely in only the way somebody poorer than their neighbors can be. Even for Tupelo, Mississippi, the Presley's were poor."

—Local hardware store manager, **F.L. Bobo**

"Vernon Presley didn't have the money to pay the $15 birth-delivery fee. Welfare went and took care of it."

—**Travis Smith**, Gladys Presley's brother

"Some say Elvis was lonesome because he was an only child. That wasn't it. And it wasn't like he didn't have relatives and cousins. He was just… apart. By circumstance and by choice."

—Classmate **Leroy Green**

"He was a sad, shy boy."

—Classmate **Kenneth Holditch**

"Elvis was a loner. He liked people. But he was quiet."

—Classmate from the second through fifth grades **Elois Bedford**

"Elvis always seemed to me to be very, very sad."

—**Ann Finch**, friend of EP from 1960-'62

"His mother Gladys was the one person who made him feel he was special. Elvis Aron was born half an hour after his twin brother Jesse Garon was born dead. Gladys willed Elvis to live and she willed him to believe in himself."

—Columnist **Joyce Haber**

"The doctor didn't know Gladys was pregnant with twins, but she did. She'd picked out the rhyming names for her boys… As Elvis grew up she often told him that the twin who survived inherited all the strength of both."

—Cousin **Billy Smith**

"Gladys intended his middle name as Aron, and that's what it says on the birth certificate. But Elvis had a fear of being unusual. He wanted to be special, not unusual. So, he later changed the spelling to the more conformist Aaron."

—Author **C. David Heymann**

"Apparently he was an adorable child. At two he clambered up onto the church choir's platform and tried to sing along without knowing the words. At three when his father was in jail for check-forging Elvis would comfort his mother by climbing up and patting her on the head and saying, 'There, there, my little baby.'"

—Magazine editor **Ingrid Sischy**

"Elvis often took me to visit Jesse's grave. The idea of twins captured his imagination. Maybe it made him feel less alone… We would go there, and Elvis would… talk a little to Jesse, and after the visit he was always lifted in his spirits."

—Childhood friend **James Ausborn**

"The family structure of a strong-willed, dominant mother with a quiescent, soft-spoken father, from a working-class, deeply religious background, with little money to spare is the same basic framework, albeit played out in different social settings, which produced Frank Sinatra, Hank Williams, Johnnie [sic] Ray and Elvis Presley."

—Author **Jonny [sic] Whiteside**

"Elvis was fragile at birth and Gladys was terrified about his health and mortality. She kept him very close... Vernon wasn't as close or affectionate, and sometimes he would drink too much. Sometimes he'd pick a fight with Gladys. It wasn't easy on young Elvis."

—*Teen Bag* editor **Lil Smith**

"Vernon was handsome. That's what drew Gladys Love Smith to him. Her dad died when she was 19 and she helped support the family. She ran a sewing machine in a garment factory, a 12-hour workday for two dollars a day... Vernon was a loafer, no ambition, out for a good time.

"When Gladys met him at church she felt she was finally entitled to a good time herself. She loved music and dancing. She was much livelier than he was... Two months later they eloped."

—Songwriter and Radio and TV reporter **Ruth Batchelor**

"Vernon couldn't afford the three-dollar wedding license and he was underage and he and Gladys had no place to live. They got married anyway. Gladys was four years older than Vernon and headstrong... A year and a half later they had Elvis."

—EP's uncle **Travis Smith**

7

Boze Hadleigh

"Vernon's gotten a bad rap, I think. It's true he couldn't hold onto a job long, but he had chronic back problems… Gladys was no saint. Her love for her son was partly a selfish thing, for her own sake… She doted on Elvis constantly, a smothering kind of affection."
—Longtime family friend **Lamar Fike**

"Elvis was the glue holding that little family together. After Vernon got out of jail early [he served eight months of a three-year sentence] as a 'hardship case,' relations between he and Gladys grew strained. He found work harder to get as a 'jailbird.' So the family started moving around a lot."
—Columnist **Lee Graham**

"Soon after Vernon returned from prison all three Presleys began having trouble sleeping. Gladys's cousin Leona recalls Elvis began sleepwalking. He continued sleepwalking for a number of years, and he continued having trouble sleeping throughout his entire life."
—Writer **John Micklos Jr.**

"In school Elvis grew more introverted as school kids teased him about being poor and then the son of a 'con.' That made his mother even more protective. Elvis told me how one time when a bunch of boys ganged up on him as he walked home from school Gladys jumped out from the front porch and scared the boys off with a broom."
—Musician **Carvell Lee Ausborn**, aka **Mississippi Slim**

"Elvis Presley was rarely or possibly never seen in denim except in a movie role. Denim and blue jeans were laborers' clothes. There was a stigma of poverty and the lower-class to them. As an adult Elvis avoided wearing fabric which held bad memories and shame."
—Hollywood costume designer **Irene Sharaff**

"In his sixth-grade class photo Elvis was the only kid wearing overalls. He put a smile on the situation but years later he not only wouldn't wear overalls or denim jeans, he didn't want the people around him to wear them."
—Friend **James Ausborn**

"I'd tramp all over town looking for so much as a single room. I'd find one, and first thing they would ask is, 'You got any children?' And I'd say I had a little boy. Then they'd shut the door."
—**Vernon Presley**, after moving to Memphis in 1943 to work in a munitions factory and hoping to relocate his wife and son from Tupelo, Mississippi

"About two years after Tupelo got its first radio station, where I was the first announcer, Elvis Presley, about eight years of age, started showing up at our weekly amateur-hour show, *Saturday Jamboree*... Locals could play or sing just by showing up, first come, first served.

"Lots of kids showed up, but the Presley boy was one of the most frequent and determined. It was as if he had nothing in his life or head but music."
—**Charlie Boren** of Radio WELO

"When Elvis had a big hit with 'Hound Dog' I remembered one of his favorite songs he used to sing. 'Old Shep' was a tearjerker about a boy and his dog. He sang it on radio whenever he could... he didn't limit himself to one type of song or music. He developed a wide repertoire, the better to be able to eventually make a hit with something or other!"

—**Mississippi Slim**

"The singing came first. Young Elvis loved to sing. But other kids he knew who could play guitar wouldn't accompany him. So eventually he got a guitar so he could accompany himself."

—Comedian and Grand Ole Opry star
Minnie Pearl

"What Elvis saved up for was to buy a rifle. His mother was against it. Anyway he didn't have the money for a rifle. Gladys said she'd make up the difference if he bought a guitar. But not a rifle."

—**Cousin Billy Smith**

"The guitar was more Gladys's idea. Elvis wanted a bicycle but he didn't have enough money. Gladys urged him to buy a guitar, and she'd help pay for it. 'Wouldn't you rather have the guitar?' she said. 'It would help you with your singing, and everyone does enjoy hearing you sing.'"

—Gladys's cousin **Corinne Richards Tate**

"If Elvis thought owning a guitar and bringing it to school would make him more popular, it didn't work... some students ridiculed him for playing 'hillbilly' music with it. But he did sing as often as he could, including in school, and he often told his classmates that some day he would sing at the Grand Ole Opry."

—Classmate **Leroy Green**

"Gladys Presley did her best to boost him, but I don't think Elvis would have had much self-confidence at all if it wasn't for his music... His looks? Some already considered him a dreamboat, but Elvis wasn't so sure. If he ever thought he was sexy, it was while he was singing."

—EP's ninth-grade homeroom teacher
Susie Johnson

"As he grew older, Elvis experimented with individuality. He often wore pink shirts and black pants... His hair was longer than most boys' hair. He slicked and shaped it with Vaseline and hair tonic. He also wore sideburns."

—**Bernard Lansky** of Lansky Brothers,
a clothing store young EP patronized

"Elvis was just so different. All the other guys were like replicas of their dads... I think he knew he was different. I knew the first time I met him that he was not like other people."

—Dixie Locke, EP's 1954 girlfriend

"When Elvis wanted to try out for the football team the coach refused, said cut your hair and then you can try out. Elvis decided to keep his hair... Then a gang of boys got Elvis into a corner and threatened to cut off his hair. I was big, I played football, so I got in there and told the guys to lay off. They backed right off."

—**Bobby "Red" West**, who became a friend
and then a bodyguard to EP

"It's true, Elvis never forgot what I did. But that cut two ways. When he became a star he didn't want people thinking I could still whup him. Not that I ever said I could, but I knew I could... He had little ways of pretending he was stronger, sometimes put-downs. Like half-joking, but put-downs.

That macho insecure worrying thing was part of him... like when we did karate, he'd get so intense... trying to prove something to everyone—but mostly himself."

—Red West

"Elvis was always real hyper. He would run and play so hard, he'd just wear himself out."

—Cousin **Harold Lloyd**

"In 1948 the reunited Presleys moved up to Memphis with some relatives. But they all lived in a small house, seven people sharing one bathroom... Finding work there wasn't easy. When they were forced to go on welfare Gladys felt very ashamed."

—Pastor and guitar player **Frank Smith**

"What it came down to was while Elvis was still in school, he took a full-time job after neither of his parents could get a job. So his grades, average to begin with, suffered and he was falling asleep in class. Finally, his counselor called in his folks and declared Elvis had to decide between work and school.

"He and Gladys chose school, and Elvis got to graduate high school—the first Presley to earn a diploma."

—Memphis friend **Buzzy Forbess** (sic)

"Cook, eat, and sleep in one room. Share bath. No privacy... Need Housing. Persons interviewed are Mrs. Presley and son. Nice boy. They seem very nice and deserving."

—Notes taken by Memphis Housing Authority's
Jane Richardson in June, 1949,
when the Presleys applied to move
into public housing after Vernon found a job

"Elvis entered numerous singing contests. Sometimes he'd win a prize. But even if it was only fifth place, he kept at it. It wasn't solely about talent. Others had talent, looks, even charisma, but sooner or later they gave up. Elvis didn't."

—Hollywood manager-producer **Sandy Gallin**

"Elvis, put down that git-ar. It's gonna be the ruination of you. You better make up your mind what you're gonna do."

—**Gladys Tipler**, co-owner of Crown Electric,
for whom EP drove a truck, often carrying
his guitar in the vehicle

"Excepting music, Elvis' other big interest was girls... and he liked them young. When he was 19 Elvis started going to a particular church in Memphis where he met a 14-year-old named Dixie. He gave her his high school ring and they went out together for two years."

—Columnist Lloyd Shearer

"When he was 14, Elvis went to work at the United Paint Company. At 15, he got hired part-time at a cinema but was fired for not doing his work and watching movies instead... At 16, he had a night-shift job at a metal products company as a sweeper... Music was Elvis' hobby. It became his salvation."

—TV host and producer **Dick Clark**

"The day before his 18th birthday the family was evicted from their home in Memphis, a major disgrace at the time. Vern took it in his stride but Gladys and Elvis were mortified... About three months later they had to move again... It became Elvis' mission in life to earn money for his family."

—Instructor and author **Eric Rofes**

"Vernon Presley wasn't ambitious till Elvis made it big. He was willing to just get by, by whatever means... Gladys was ambitious for her son but couldn't do much about it... She was rather pretty and lively in earlier years—I think life with Vern and poverty aged her. She found solace in Elvis, in overeating and drinking."

—childhood classmate **Kenneth Holditch**

"It's not surprising, considering, to learn both Elvis Presley's parents were alcoholic. What's surprising is how seldom it's mentioned in his life story... as opposed to, say, Carol Burnett's parents or Mary Tyler Moore's parents, etc."

—*Movieline* editor **Ed Margulies**

"I think [Gladys Presley] really had trouble as his popularity grew. It grew hard for her to let everybody have him. I had the same feelings. He did not belong to us anymore."

—Girlfriend **Dixie Locke**

"Elvis held that monogamy was for womenfolk. No matter what he had at home, on the road he had endless groupies... After he broke through big-time in 1955 he decided he didn't want a commitment, so he broke with Dixie. His excuse was she'd been unfaithful while he was on the road, even though the exact opposite was true."

—Uncle **Vester Presley**

"Of course, Elvis eventually quit trucking to give all his time to singing and performing... He still got a lot of derision... there were always people ready to make fun of his clothes or his performance physicality. But the reaction of most audiences, above all the girls, kept his hopes high."

—Former singer **Merv Griffin**

"You ain't goin' nowhere, son. You ought to go back to drivin' a truck."

—**Jim Denny**, Grand Ole Opry manager
who in 1954 fired Elvis
after a single performance

"Who knows what else would have become of him? Elvis didn't hold down any job very long. He worked for Precision Tool a month or so... he was studying to be an electrician, then worked for Crown Electric under a year and a half.

"Lucky he didn't let go of his interest in singing. Or have a dad in whose footsteps he could follow."

—*Tiger Beat* editor **Ralph Benner**

"Elvis was hoping very hard for a career in music. But he avoided putting all his eggs in one basket. He knew the odds. By day he drove a truck and by night he was studying to be an electrician."

—Cousin **Billy Smith**

"After stardom happened, Elvis, who used to say he wasn't anyone real special, began saying and repeating that he always had faith he'd become a star… that God wouldn't let him down… it was his destiny and that kind of thing."

—**Sonny West** (Red's cousin),
member of EP's entourage,
the "Memphis mafia"

"Lots of celebrities do commercials. On the way up or when they're stars… Elvis did one, total. In 1955, for Southern Made Donuts… They weren't the best-tasting."

—Comedian **Nipsey Russell**,
one-time opening act for EP

"They say Elvis developed a pretty hard shell… probably had to. But back then he was pretty vulnerable."

—Classmate **Shirley Henderson**

"That comment he received after appearing at the Grand Ole Opry broke Elvis' hopeful heart. He left Nashville with tears in his eyes."

—EP biographer **Steven Zmijewsky**

"The country-music establishment was always pretty narrow… While a newcomer, Elvis Presley was often identified with country music, yet they didn't want any part of him. They said he 'warped' or 'vulgarized' their music… Decades later when Olivia Newton-John was winning country-music awards they tried to get her to give them back because she wasn't American."

—Jazz singer **Anita O'Day**

"There is a direct performance line between Al Jolson, Johnnie Ray, and Elvis Presley. Jolson was so expansive and emotional that he often had to sing on stage in blackface. It freed him from being stifled within what was acceptable for a white man. Ray, who was secretly gay, was also expressive.

"Ray became a superstar about four years before Elvis. He was the first white popular singer to stand at a piano, to remove a mic from its stand and prowl the stage with it, to fall to his knees during a song without ethnic makeup, etc. Elvis copied much of this… and being prettier and straighter, he lasted longer."

—Music historian **Deborah Lavi**

"The marketing people have changed the story, now they only say it was Bill Haley & the Comets who was the big early [rock 'n roll] influence, before Elvis Presley… I consider Johnnie Ray to be the father of rock 'n roll… But now they never mention Johnnie Ray, and I don't understand it—because *I was there, Charlie*, you know?"

—**Tony Bennett**

"In 1953 when Sam Phillips paced his Memphis Sun Studio's floor and told secretary Marion Keisker, 'If I could only find a white man who sang like a Negro, I'd make a million dollars,' he meant 'another Johnnie Ray'—albeit a heterosexual model of same."

—Johnnie Ray biographer **Jonny Whiteside**

"Elvis soon learned from all the loud disapproval and censure that his physical moves were too much for the Establishment and couldn't continue indefinitely. They earned him attention and took him far, but when he reached the top he knew to tone his act down. He wanted to remain up there and be nationally popular, not just with teens and rebels. Teens don't do the hiring or pay the salaries."

—Singer **George Michael**

"Anyone who lasts in show business can't remain too controversial for too long."

—**Kurt Cobain**

"You'll notice that the left side of Elvis' body is more… active. It was his left leg that jerked and twitched so sexily. And his generous mouth would sneer and curl on the left side."

—Co-star **Hope Lange** (*Wild in the Country*)

"It's fortunate for Elvis he was physically uninhibited. He knew his voice wasn't extraordinary… that his looks and S.A. [sex appeal] would make the difference."

—**Kay Medford** (*Bye Bye Birdie* on Broadway)

"Put it this way: Roy Orbison was definitely more talented than Presley. Talent's a great thing. But physical appeal is a crucial thing."

—**Frank Barron**, editor of *The Hollywood Reporter*

"Poor guy. Memphis, in summer of 1954 he was my opening act. Audiences came to hear me, and Elvis Presley sang 'Blue Moon of Kentucky.' He heard noises coming from the audience and thought he was being booed. He came offa the stage so low you didn't know to laugh or cry for him. But they just told him go back out there and do an encore—the audience wanted him back."

—Singer **Slim Whitman**

"In 1954 record producer Sam Phillips brought together singer Elvis Presley, guitarist Scotty Moore and bass player Bill Black. They began recording together and touring the region. A year later, after Elvis signed with Colonel Tom Parker, the Sun contract was sold to RCA, which remained Elvis' lifelong record label. It enabled him to move from a regional hit to a national hit."

—Librarian and writer **Marilyn Collins**

"In 1954 I had a cousin living in Memphis. He had a radio; no TV yet. The first DJ to ever play an Elvis Presley record on radio was on Memphis station WHBQ. Same day, this singer with the funny first name was interviewed by the DJ. My cousin said he was an okay singer but not so good talking. What made the key difference was TV—Presley was a visual sensation."

—Cable-TV talk host **Skip E. Lowe**

"As Elvis admitted, his voice was good enough but not that special. It's what he did with it… accompanied by his body language, his good looks, his flirty facial expressions… it was the whole package that appealed—and then some."

—**Carrie Fisher**

"In 1954 Elvis got himself a manager [Scotty Moore]… 1955 he signs with Bob Neal to be his manager. Bob

Boze Hadleigh

would receive 15 percent of Elvis' income, compared to an agent's 10 percent. Weeks later, Bob Neal gets 'Colonel' Tom Parker's help in booking Elvis at Carlsbad, New Mexico. He would pay dearly for that 'help.'

Months after that, Neal and Parker have a chat about Elvis' career. Then, in July 1955, Parker meets Elvis in person and is smitten—spell it $mitten... he sees a green, green future for both of them, and at much more than just 15 percent for himself.

Parker starts courting Elvis, then courts his parents, it's 1956, Bob Neal's out of the picture... and Parker's in to stay... and stay... and to way outlive his golden goose."
—ICM agent **Ed Limato**

"Yeah, 1955, right? I was touring overseas, then I return to the U.S. and I don't know what's been going on. But almost the first thing the reporters ask when I arrive at the airport is about this new singer who's scored so big and so fast. And innocently I say, 'What's an Elvis Presley?' A mistake, because then they report it as sour grapes on my part."

—Johnnie Ray

"His name was so unusual that when he started out it sometimes got misspelled Alvis. Or Elves. Sometimes the last name too... Parsley, even."
—Mexican-American EP "interpreter" and musician **El Vez**

"In 1956 Elvis' manager signed with an outfit called Special Projects to manufacture 188 saleable Elvis items. Everything from glow-in-the-dark portraits, bookends, hair brushes, underwear—that was controversial—stuffed hound dogs, colognes, mittens, purses, soft drinks, you name it. Parker was the first to make tie-in merchandising a big business."

—Hollywood business manager
A. Morgan Maree

"I wore lipstick sometimes and liked one of the Elvis lipsticks. They called it Tutti Frutti Red. But *I* made that song famous, it was *mine*... Mr. Presley, later on, he stops singing my song because he says it *embarrasses* him. Well, I'm man enough *not* to be embarrassed."

—Singer-songwriter **Little Richard**
(the other lipstick colors were Heartbreak
Hotel Pink and Hound Dog Orange)

"By the 1960s in the United States they were constantly misspelling my name to match Elvis Presley!"

—French actress **Micheline Preslé** (no "y")

"At the start, he was more about country and rhythm-and-blues and gospel music than rock 'n roll. The latter category was new and fresh... Elvis didn't enjoy being called a hick singer who used to drive a truck."

—EP's movie director **Hal Kanter**

"He's okay if you like hillbilly music."

—Singer **Vic Damone** on the Southern vocalist
then best known for touring the South with his
band and for regular appearances on the weekly
Louisiana Hayride radio show

"A Howling Hillbilly Success"

—Headline in *Life* magazine,
EP's first national magazine spread

"Elvis has left the building."
>   —*Louisiana Hayride* announcer's statement,
>   meant to deter rowdy teenage audiences
>   who might otherwise seek the singer backstage

"Driving a truck is nothing to be ashamed of. Trucks deliver all the food and so much of everything else... But when you've been a truck driver and you have some looks and then you become famous, it takes many years for reporters to stop judging you as a not-too-smart pretty-boy who drove a truck and then got lucky. It happened to me and it happened to Elvis."

—Rock Hudson

"Elvis' first released record was 'That's All Right, Mama.' It came out in August, 1954, and did well—when and where it was allowed to play. Radio stations in assorted Southern states refused to play it because it 'sounded too black.'"

—Singer **Della Reese**

"The first Elvis record to appear on any national chart was in mid July, 1955, titled 'Baby, Let's Play House.' The title was more than a little provocative at the time."

—Musical orchestrator **Paul Buckmaster**

"Elvis' 1955 hit record made no difference in Las Vegas. At the New Frontier Hotel he was billed as 'Elvis Presley—the Atomic Powered Singer,' a reference to Johnnie Ray, who was often called 'The Atomic Ray.' After Elvis laid an egg the billing was changed overnight to 'Freddy Martin's Orchestra, also Elvis Presley.'

Meanwhile, directly across the Strip, Johnnie Ray was enjoying a very successful run at the Desert Inn. Elvis often went to see him perform."
—Australian musicologist **Van Davies**

"After Elvis was through with motion pictures and vice versa, he would go watch Tom Jones in performance in Las Vegas. Tom Jones was a huge new success there… the two eventually became friends... He didn't realize Presley was doing research… he wanted his return to Vegas to be a triumph. He had no intention of flopping there twice."
—Las Vegas journalist **Holt Wendell**

"God bless Elvis Presley, and nothing against the man, but he seems calculated in those early rock 'n roll days… He knows what he's doing. The choreography, the moves lifted from chorus girls. He knows how he looks… he's working on it."

—Tom Jones

"On January 10, 1956, Elvis recorded his first song for RCA-Victor, 'Heartbreak Hotel,' a big success. RCA hadn't wanted him to record it—'too depressing.' It topped the charts for almost two months."
—Music publisher **Raphael Jerome**

"He sneered, dropped his eyelids and smiled out of the left side of his mouth. He used every physical trick that had come to him since his first record was released."
—Biographer **Jerry Hopkins** on EP's
January 28, 1956, appearance on the
national TV program *Showtime*,
produced by Jackie Gleason

"Some people don't criticize their elders. I don't criticize my juniors."

—Singer **Bing Crosby**, asked by his banker in Hillsborough, California, if he were an Elvis fan

"He is not my cup of tea."

—TV host **Ed Sullivan**

"By the mid 1950s television could make a star... Conservative hosts like Ed Sullivan and Arthur Godfrey determined that Presley should not become a star. They viewed him as a moral threat who encouraged promiscuity and juvenile delinquency... Sullivan declared he would never allow Elvis on his show. But Presley's popularity kept skyrocketing and it became obvious no one could prevent his stardom."

—'50s TV star **Sid Caesar**

"Subsidized sex."
—Newspaper reviewer Dr. **Ida Halpern** on EP's August 31, 1957, concert in Vancouver, Canada

"Over the years Presley made some disparaging remarks about New York City. I don't know if it was the usual hickish anti-Semitism or something to do with the big TV hosts like Godfrey and Sullivan, few if any of whom were Jewish... But he did get very defensive early on... would say, 'Those people in New York aren't gonna change me none.'"

—Agent **Frank Rio**

"Some boys were big Elvis fans but mostly it was the girls. They displayed the same frenzied reaction that later greeted the Beatles. It frightened parents, churches and the government… it didn't exactly please the boyfriends."

—Music historian **Charlene Held**

"Elvis Presley's success earned him thousands of enemies in the shape of his fans' boyfriends. To them he was an arrogant and rich thief of their girls' loyalty and affections… Individually and sometimes in gangs, young men would try to waylay Elvis after a show. Bodyguards became a permanent part of his life."

—Songwriter **Sammy Cahn**

"It was murder for us as Beatles at the height of the hysteria. But there were four of us to share it. Elvis was on his own. There was only him. It must have been impossible."

—**John Lennon**

"When Elvis finally appeared on Mr. Sullivan's show, he absented himself that week. Charles was the guest host. He had a crush on Elvis, who ultimately guested thrice on the Sullivan show… The third time [in 1957] was the famous one that censored him from the waist down."

—**Elsa Lanchester**, wife of closeted movie star Charles Laughton

"[He] behaves like a sex maniac in public."

—Banjoist and bandleader **Eddie Condon**

"American boy singers during the political witch-hunt era were not supposed to be overtly sexy. Gentlemen first and last. Understandably, some established singers were jealous of Presley's out-there style."

—**Alan Meltzer**, Broadway press agent

"Presley and his frustration of voodoo and defiance have become symbols in our country, and we are sorry to come upon Ed Sullivan in the role of promoter. Your Catholic viewers, Mr. Sullivan, are angry."

—*The Catholic Sun*

"From what I've heard, I'm not sure I'd want my children to see him."

—Evangelist **Billy Graham**

"… a whirling dervish of sex."

—Reverend **Charles Howard Graff**
of St. John's Episcopal Church

"I remember when America's preachers were cursing Elvis Presley. Ridiculous. Now [in the 1990s] I hear there's something called the Presbyterian Church of the Divine Elvis. Ridiculous."

—**Roger Smith**,
Ann-Margret's husband and manager

"Elvis Presley has pizzaz. He's a spectacle to behold and he makes you feel livelier than when you sat down."

—Singer **Kay Starr**

"So far as teenagers are concerned, Elvis is what I call a safety valve. They scream, holler and let go of their emotions when they see him perform."

—**David Weisbart**, producer of EP's first film and of
Rebel Without a Cause

"Jimmy Dean and Elvis Presley were the two real teen idols that emerged during the '50s. Dean's impact was more impressive because he's still remembered after only three movies—and he didn't sing."
—Composer/lyricist **Michael Friedman**

"Everyone thinks Elvis TV-debuted on Ed Sullivan. But before that he did Milton Berle, Steve Allen and pert near any TV show his manager was allowed to get him on. 'Course after he moved into movin' pictures the Colonel wouldn't allow Elvis on TV nohow."
—Self-described "country-hick performer"
Pat Buttram (TV's *Green Acres*)

"Elvis was so controversial that when Steve Allen agreed to have him on, he laid down the condition that Elvis look and behave properly. He had to wear a white tuxedo and when he sang his new hit 'Hound Dog' it wasn't to a female, it was sung to an actual hound dog seated on a stool. Elvis and his fans were incensed, but getting on TV was worth it, professionally."
—TV producer **George Schlatter**

"If his 'entertainment' could be confined to records it might not be too bad an influence on the young, but unfortunately Presley makes personal appearances... If the agencies—TV and other—would stop handling such nauseating stuff, all the Presleys of our land would soon be swallowed in the oblivion they deserve."
—The Catholic weekly magazine *America*

"Gladys Presley felt keenly the venom aimed at her son. It hurt and embarrassed her... [and] made her afeared

[sic] for his future and safety… She told Vernon, Elvis might not live out a full lifespan on account of some deranged fan or enemy."

—Early EP friend **Mississippi Slim**

"After Elvis bought Graceland in 1957 for $40,000 cash Gladys still wasn't happy. She felt self-conscious when she hung the laundry out on the clothes line and people stared or fans stole articles of male clothing… Elvis had to put in a brick wall around the house, for privacy… Graceland was named after the great-aunt of the woman for whom it was built."

—EP fan club vice-president **Abel Torrano**

"The Presley family bought Graceland for $102,500… any $100,000 house then was a mansion. The average U.S. annual wage in 1957 was $3,641.72."

—**Harrison Freedman**, economics professor and clarinetist

"I'm miserable. I'm guarded. I can't go buy my own groceries. I can't go to the movies. I can't see my neighbors. I'm the most miserable woman in the world."

—**Gladys Presley** to a friend, quoted in *Elvis and Gladys* by Elaine Dundy

"Several neighbors were unhappy about the Presleys moving into Graceland. Some of them got up a petition declaring that the family's presence was lowering property values in that affluent area… A public-nuisance lawsuit was filed against Elvis and his family but the judge threw it out."

—Rock 'n roll historian **Maria Martin**

"One of the newly rich Elvis' favorite purchases was his pink-and-white Cadillac. He also bought numerous shirts in his favorite colors, pink and black… He bought his mother a pink Cadillac, but she didn't like to drive."
—Country comedian **Minnie Pearl**

"Elvis was particularly worried about his mother. Her health was poor and although Elvis never said so, insiders said she'd become an alcoholic, which further affected her health… I don't think he would have married any girl while his mama was still alive."
—**Natalie Wood**, who met EP in 1955

"1956 was Elvis Presley's *annus mirabilis*. He had four top-of-the-charts songs that stayed and stayed up there… a record unbroken until 1964 when the Beatles charted five out of the top five songs."
—Music instructor **Larry Shelly**

"No artist had ever exploded on the scene with the volcanic impact of Elvis Presley in 1956, and no manager before Tom Parker had ever been so brilliantly or blatantly capitalistic."
—EP biographer **Alanna Nash**

"Who else but Elvis could take an old forgotten Civil War song, 'Aura Lee,' and turn it into the huge hit vocal 'Love Me Tender.'"
—Pianist and composer **Greg Schreiner**

"They renamed Elvis' first movie, *Love Me Tender*, after the song. It was going to be called *The Reno Brothers*. He played the youngest of four brothers and was third-billed. The leading man was Richard Egan... Elvis dies in the end so that Richard can marry the leading lady after she becomes a widow. It was a western with a handful of songs, set during the Civil War."

—**Mildred Dunnock**, who played EP's mother

"Is it a sausage?... Is it a Walt Disney goldfish?... Is it a corpse? The face just hangs there, limp and white with its little drop-seat mouth. But suddenly the figure comes to life. The lips part, the eyes half close, the clutched guitar begins to undulate back and forth in an uncomfortably suggestive manner. And wham! The midsection of the body jolts forward to bump and grind... boogie and hillbilly rock 'n roll and something known only to Elvis and his Pelvis."

—*Time* **Magazine review** of EP's movie debut

"In his first movie Elvis kept his natural hair color, dark blond. The male lead had dark hair. So did most leading men, and one whom Elvis particularly admired was black-haired Tony Curtis [*né* Bernard Schwartz]. He may have copied him... Blond leading men were few and far between until the 1960s and Robert Redford."

—Columnist **Dorothy Manners**

"Possibly Elvis Presley believed dyeing his hair black made him appear more masculine and mature."

—Modeling agency owner **Nina Blanchard**

"Mr. Presley's skill lies in another direction. He is a rock-and-roll variation of... the hootchy-kootchy. His one specialty is an accented movement of the body that heretofore has been primarily identified with the repertoire of the blonde bombshells of the burlesque runway."

—*New York Times* TV critic **Jack Gould**,
dismissing EP's singing

"He can't sing a lick, makes up for vocal shortcomings with the weirdest and plainly planned suggestive animation short of an aborigine's mating dance."

—Critic **Jack O'Brien** of the
New York Journal-American

"When he began in movies Elvis had no idea if he'd be acceptable to the wider audience. It takes far more fans to be a movie star than to be a hit singer… He did feel a bit insecure about his lightish hair—he was a singer, and singing and dancing aren't the most butch things you can do in movies... For the screen Elvis wanted something darker… and to fit in with male stars he looked up to like Bob Mitchum, Rock Hudson and Tony Curtis."

—**Robert D. Webb**, EP's first movie director

"Elvis could have dyed his hair brown and looked fantastic and more natural. But he chose jet black. Also eyeliner. The effect, intended or not, was to make his skin look even whiter. Whether that had anything to do with his Southern background or mindset, I don't know."

—Celebrity makeup artist **Way Bandy**

"Elvis did a Christmas album in 1957 that got into trouble because of the religious aspect. Many radio stations wouldn't play Elvis Presley singing traditional Christmas songs… One non-traditional song was Irving Berlin's 'White Christmas.' Berlin himself asked radio stations to not play Elvis' version, which he believed was contrary to the spirit of Christmas."

—Songwriter **Hugh Martin**

"If any further proof were needed that what Elvis offers is not basically music but a sex show, it was proved last night."

—Critic **Dick Williams** in the *Los Angeles Mirror-News* after the first night of EP's debut live performance in Hollywood in October, 1957

"The Los Angeles Vice Squad told Tom Parker that Elvis needed to tone down the [October, 1957, Hollywood] show for the second night. Otherwise he might go to jail for indecency. The police actually showed up with movie cameras to film the second show. If Elvis did anything obscene, they would have proof on tape. The show that night was much tamer."

—EP biographer **John Micklos Jr.**

"I remember from the way some critics reviewed Elvis' early concerts, you'd have thought sex was being performed onstage. Yet it was Elvis and nobody else. Which in a way didn't mean there was no sex at all onstage..."

—Actress **Sandra Dee**

"On the way up, it wasn't Elvis alone. He had a band, he had competent musicians. As a guitarist he wasn't that proficient. The two musicians who toured extensively with him when he was breaking through were Scotty Moore and Bill Black. They were integral to the Elvis sound.

"But each man only earned $100 a week, $200 while on the road. They had to pay all their own traveling expenses and the situation was becoming lopsided. Elvis often earned $7,500 a week. In the fall of 1957, they finally quit."

—Rock 'n roll historian **John Gerold Frank**

"Elvis is the star and we know it. I didn't expect to get rich on this… but I did expect to do better than I have and to make a good living for my family."

—Scotty Moore

"They'd been a trio, with Presley the vocalist… First they all stopped sharing, then the two men's percentage decreased, then they were put on salary rather than receiving a percentage. To top it off, Scotty Moore and Bill Black hadn't been given a raise in two years. It was indecently unfair.

Elvis told Scotty he just left the business side of things to the Colonel, his manager. The two men had stayed because they earned more as musicians than if they'd been driving trucks."

—Hollywood money manager **A. Morgan Maree**

"When Bill and Scotty left Elvis he was outraged at their 'betrayal'… I think secretly he was scared, unsure if he could make it solo. They'd helped shape the Elvis sound, a blend of country and blues… Weeks after they quit, Scotty and Bill were induced to come back; Elvis still needed them. But they were paid a flat rate per show. Scotty said it stuck in his craw but as a family man he needed the income."

—Singer/pianist **Buddy Greco**

"The two provided virtually all the music. Elvis wore his guitar on stage but mostly he sang and postured and gyrated and all the rest of it… Bill eventually left for good, but Scotty accompanied Elvis off and on until 1969. Elvis had no more partners, just an employee who knew to toe the line."

—Actor and early EP friend **Nick Adams**

"Elvis had peer relationships with fellow musicians and people in general. Until he hit the top. Then things changed. Or rather, he did. No more peer relationships. Except with the Colonel, who held the upper hand—the one with the money in it."

—**Mimi Farina**, folk singer
and sister of Joan Baez

"He was devastated when he found out he was going to be drafted. 'Why me?' Elvis kept asking. He cried tears over it. He was just sure after two years away his fans would pledge their allegiance to some new singer, some newer star. He said they was fickle like that and he'd be washed up when he came back to bein' a civilian."

—Friend **Lamar Fike**

"When Elvis had his hair cut by an army barber the Colonel turned it into a big photo op… *Time* said Elvis' hair was swimming with sweat and goose grease. The Colonel wasn't allowed to save the hair. He just shook his head and said, 'I know a lot of people who would pay a lot of money for that hair!'"

—Cousin **Billy Smith**

"For three days a media parade with Colonel Tom as Grand Marshall followed Elvis through the induction process."

—*Life* Magazine

"While Elvis was in mourning for himself the Colonel was enjoying all the publicity surrounding Elvis being drafted. With his hat tilted at a jaunty angle, he chatted away with reporters and army brass, handed out balloons advertising Elvis' latest movie, and kept busy devising schemes to keep Elvis' name before the public."

—Columnist **Richard Gully**

"Fellow privates teased Elvis and asked if he missed his teddy bear, on account of that hit song. Elvis had never been much for teddy bears, though the song resulted in his receiving hundreds of them. What he really missed was his mom."

—EP fan club member **Dee Dee Hafner**

"His barracks mates reacted to Elvis in different ways but they did get used to him. In the army he couldn't play at being a celebrity. Except he did buy each of them a spare uniform and sometimes paid another soldier 20 bucks to take over his KP duty. Could be Elvis didn't feel he could make friends without buying their friendship."

—Military historian **Harlan Andrews**

"Elvis was posted to Fort Hood [Texas] but whenever he could get away from the base he'd come over to my house in Waco. I remember when he called his mother and… for a solid hour they were crying, weeping, moaning on the telephone. Not hardly a word was spoken."

—Friend **Eddie Fadal**

"Gladys and Elvis always had pet names for each other. She called him, for instance, Baby or Naughty or Ageless… one of his favorites for her was Satnin, the name of a brand of lard that was advertised as 'chubby, round and comfortable.'"

—Uncle **Travis Smith**

"As often as not, Elvis shared his mother's bed, growing up. When his father was away that's where he usually slept. Of course it was innocent but it didn't say much for Gladys's desire to not keep her only child emotionally over-dependent on her. Such parenting stems from adult immaturity, even selfishness."

—Psychologist **Betty Berzon**

"Elvis was in basic training when he got word his mother's health had worsened. She was already a heavy drinker, overweight and suffering from hepatitis. He became frantic and threatened to go AWOL if he didn't get an emergency furlough, which was finally granted. He had two days with her before she died" [at 46].

—Newspaper publisher **Henry McClurg**

"Wearing a white frilled shirt his mother had often admired, he sat with his father on the steps of Graceland and cried inconsolably… When her body was laid in its

grave, Elvis tried to leap in after it. For days he clutched her pink housecoat to his breast and kissed it lovingly. One witness called it 'the most pitiful sight you ever saw.'"
—Journalist **Charles Hirshberg**

"He changed completely [after Gladys's death]. He didn't seem like Elvis ever again."
—EP's aunt **Lillian Mann Smith**

"He was a mama's boy."
—**Barbara Pittman**,
singer with Sun Records

"There was a Chinese saying Elvis told me he liked: Children are not different than their mother."
—**Dolores del Rio**, who played his
mother in *Flaming Star* (1960)

"Elvis never really got over his mother's death."
—Stepbrother **Rick Stanley**

"He was white as a sheet. He started to sob this kind of unearthly sound."
—**Billy Smith**, about his cousin's mourning

"When you chronicle the demise of Elvis Presley you have to realize that the tilt started when Gladys died. That was the most devastating thing that ever happened to him. He would never be the same."
—**Lamar Fike**, member of EP's entourage

"After the army… he started taking all this medicine— the pills, the tranquilizers and sleeping medication like

Boze Hadleigh

the doctor had him on and prescribed to him immediately following Gladys's death."
　　　　　　　—**Anita Wood**, an early girlfriend

"Elvis loved his father. The problem was Vernon, not Elvis… Vernon was basically jealous of Elvis. As the years went by, the normal father-son roles were reversed. Elvis became the provider."
　　　　　　　—**Marty Lacker**, part of the "Memphis mafia"

"I picked up on Elvis' attitude toward Vernon. I didn't particularly care for him either. I thought he was pretty selfish and just along for the ride. I don't think he was any kind of a father for Elvis. There seemed to be a big vacuum there."
　　　　　　　—**Ann Finch**, a friend of EP from 1960 to '62

"Elvis was sailing to Germany for an 18-month posting. Colonel Parker invited photographers, reporters and some 2,000 fans to the Brooklyn pier. Elvis' mother was dead and he was at an emotional low over that and his immediate future.

"Nevertheless a military band was on hand to play 'Tutti Frutti' while Elvis had to walk up the gangplank eight times for the photographers, carrying a heavy duffel bag that didn't belong to him. Finally, the U.S.S. General Randall set sail across the Atlantic to the tune of 'Don't Be Cruel.'"
　　　　　　　—Columnist **Lee Graham**

"Something the Colonel didn't arrange was for Elvis and Vernon to find romance in Germany… With Gladys Presley gone, Elvis' father joined his son there.

Also joining him were Elvis' grandmother Minnie Mae as sort of a housekeeper and his pals Red West and Lamar Fike.

"West often picked fights with locals in beer gardens and Minnie Mae was at loggerheads with their landlord and once attacked her with a broom handle. It was like something out of a more aggressive *Beverly Hillbillies*."

—Film historian **Carlos Clarens**

"Elvis Presley was given the privilege of living off-base with relatives and friends while in Germany. That did not endear him to most of his fellow soldiers."
—**Lotte Mueller**, waitress in Bad Neuheim, Germany, where the Presleys dwelled

"Elvis hated his life in the Third Armored Division in Germany. It was so dull and conformist compared to his recent glamorous life. He hated the boredom and, according to insiders, started taking stimulants at that time."
—United Artists music executive **Marilyn Petrone**

"Vernon Presley began dating a married woman and mother named Dee Stanley. Vernon wanted female companionship… their relationship intensified and he remarried. Elvis refused to attend the wedding.

"When they were all back in the USA and installed at Graceland Elvis grew more tolerant of his stepmother and told the press he'd always wanted a kid brother and now he had three. But relations remained somewhat strained."

—Columnist and former aide to
Jack Warner **Richard Gully**

"Elvis lost it when Dee did some unauthorized redecorating in Graceland. As far as he was concerned that was still his mother's home. He ripped down the drapes and put an angry stop to any major changes... By then Vernon was on the payroll, technically employed by his son. All one big happy family, according to publicity."

—Friend **Buzzy Forbess**

"Elvis was spending more time in Hollywood making movies. He bought a lavish place there. With more privacy than at Graceland, which housed several of his relatives and was far from the fleshpots of L.A."

—Columnist **James Bacon**

"John Lennon said going into the army killed Elvis' spirit. It did knock off some of the original Elvis... After he came out of it the sideburns were gone and his hips stopped swiveling. The Pelvis part of him went into retirement. Like he was embarrassed about it... He was wearing more suits... Some of Elvis' teenage audience felt he'd turned on them. But he was moving into Middle America's good graces and toward the older generations."

—*King Creole* co-star **Vic Morrow**

"Elvis was relieved he not only still had his career, post-military, but he was still in demand for movies... He didn't have to sweat and strain singing in live performance. He'd just go into the studio and sing the songs for a given movie soundtrack. They sold well despite their inferior quality.

"The new tamed Elvis was nowhere as exciting.

But now things were easier and more lucrative. That also meant he had more time to start developing bad habits."

—Broadway composer **Jerry Herman**

"What's near-miraculous, 'cause he was horny to a tee, is Elvis didn't father any known illegitimate kids. Rumor was, he had a low sperm count. No idea if it was true."

—Army buddy **Rex Mansfield**

"Colonel Parker was able to convince Elvis that without him he was nothing. Right off the bat he asked for and got 25 percent of Presley's earnings, later asking for and getting 50 percent... Parker kept reminding Presley how lucky he was to still be popular after the two-year interruption of his career. He emphasized that it was thanks to his persistent efforts.

"He wasn't far wrong. He had Elvis pre-record a ton of songs before his induction."

—Paramount executive **A.C. Lyles**

"What dampened Elvis' spirit was the loss of his adoring audiences. From 1961 to 1968 or '69 he didn't make public appearances, including for charity. He lost touch with the public. The public was changing... maturing, growing more sophisticated. While Elvis remained a boy-man, living an insulated, unreal and dependent lifestyle."

—Columnist **Radie Harris**

"When Elvis did come back to performing there were some anonymous threats. Sooner or later every big name gets threats, including death threats. Elvis took it too much to heart. He started getting paranoid, and it got worse... he'd pack a pistol in his boot, carry one at the small of his back... he had a pistol in the john, one in the bedroom. He started a collection. He let his paranoia blossom."

—Cinematographer **Lucien Ballard**
(*Elvis—That's the Way It Is*)

"Elvis would deny that he had bodyguards. But that's what most of the Memphis mafia were. They doubled as bodyguards and gofers... Elvis didn't feel safe on his own. You know, *entourage* in French means that which surrounds you.

"Elvis thought saying 'bodyguard' meant he couldn't defend himself. He wanted a powerful image. Karate was part of that."

—Security advisor **Howard Devane**

"While Elvis was in the army in Germany he was invited to sing for the troops. That was relayed back to the Colonel in the States. The Colonel said no way, not even for the soldiers... if they wanted to hear his 'boy' sing, they'd have to pay, just like everybody else."

—Band leader **Les Brown**

"Had he been female he'd have been accused of being ungrateful and unpatriotic... Elvis turned down requests to sing for the U.S. army in Europe and President Nixon in the White House—Nixon asked him personally."

—U.K. singer **Dusty Springfield**

"Elvis would never sing a duet or perform a free song at someone else's show, even if asked to. He was willing, however, to perform a bit of karate demonstration, like he did at Tom Jones's show at Caesar's Palace."
—Press agent **Alan Meltzer**

"Over time, Presley got more controlling. If he entertained, he always preferred it to be in his hotel suite or domain. He preferred to be in charge. He wanted to play host, with his boys around him, in a familiar setting. He didn't feel comfortable in someone else's domain, he didn't like being someone's guest."
—Singer **Mel Tormé**

"He once complained to me that he couldn't go into restaurants and not be noticed—the traditional lament of the famous man. I had to point out that the rhinestone suits he wore [in the '70s] off-stage as well as on-stage, the massive hair and sideburns and the huge dark glasses were not helping him in this area. That didn't convince him to change any of it. I think Elvis enjoyed being Elvis."
—**Tom Jones**

"Like a kid, he enjoyed play-acting. He was playing a role, and it made him feel important, so he became that role. And it completely took him over."
—Co-star **Gavin Gordon** (*Girls! Girls! Girls!*)

"I don't know if it was Gladys's influence, but as a young man Elvis was in some ways nearer a boy. He liked to attend Saturday kiddie matinees when he was 18 or 19. The rest of the audience was mainly children, from small fry to puberty. Elvis would sit and eat his popcorn and un-self-consciously laugh along with them at the cartoons and the super-hero adventure serials."

—**George Weinberg**, psychotherapist and writer

"He was a very *young* 24. I mean, he and the guys played like teenagers. They'd have water fights and chase each other through the halls and play hide-and-seek… kid stuff. So he didn't really seem older and he didn't *act* older."

—**Sandy Ferra**, a dancer at the
Hollywood Professional School
whom EP dated while she was underaged

"I recently came upon a mid-'70s photo of Elvis posed between a police chief and a police captain… wearing basically the same cap and uniform they were. It's sadly phony and juvenile. A man in middle age, playing dress-up next to actual law enforcement, pretending he has anything to do with them… and yet they indulged him."

—**Lizabeth Scott**, EP's co-star
in his second film, *Loving You Then*

"Elvis has two competing posthumous images. There's the boyish, sexy but natural Elvis. And the experienced Elvis who fell out of favor for a while but came back strong as a flashy showman and icon."

—**Emily Sisley**, psychologist and writer

"Two examples of bizarre laws are the French law prohibiting a pig to be given the name Napoleon and the Swiss law whereby it's illegal to mow one's front lawn dressed as Elvis Presley. No mention of the backyard, which is more private."

—**Jim Graham**, attorney and politician

"Elvis didn't approve of women dressing in pants. He turned off to anything slightly butch. He preferred frilly and girly… His girlfriends were instructed by one of his staff how to dress to please Elvis."

—Designer and "worst-dressed maven"
Mr. Blackwell

When she met EP "I looked like I was 13 years old… We didn't come close to having sex but I was expected to stay the night, which I didn't want to… I've read about his sexual behavior [but]… he preferred pumping to actual sex… He preferred the petting, the kissing… It was adolescent—until all of a sudden you graduated into Mother.

You were expected to take care of him, basically that's what the role was: to get him things in the middle of the night. He needed water, he needed pills, he needed Jell-O, he needed to be read to. That was what I did."

—Early '70s girlfriend **Sheila Ryan**

"It's ironic he never went to a psychiatrist because Elvis Presley had more to tell a shrink than most people would."

—*Kid Galahad* co-star **Lola Albright**

"Peter Pan, the boy who never grew up? *Elvis*."
—Journalist **Lance Loud**

PART TWO:
FAME AND THE KINGMAKER

Fame and The KingMaker

Elvis with his looks and charisma was bound to be discovered sooner or later. It was later. He wanted badly to join someone's band but received rejections. He hoped to earn money for his family by singing but it didn't amount to much and while driving a truck he studied to be an electrician. After making it to country music's celebrated Grand Ole Opry Elvis was dismissed after one performance and told "You ain't goin' nowhere, son," advised to stick to trucking. His big break was getting on and becoming a repeat guest on *Louisiana Hayride*, a Southern radio show. His bigger break was drawing the cunning attention of a man who called himself Colonel Tom Parker but was born Andreas Cornelis van Kuijk.

The "Colonel" had several secrets. For one, he was an illegal alien from Holland who'd slipped into the U.S., possibly through Canada, after fleeing his small hometown in 1929 with little more than the clothes on his back. He left it within hours of the murder of a woman there. In the States the renamed Tom Parker found work in carnivals and as a con man. Eventually he became the manager of country singer Eddy Arnold, who fired him for being too controlling. Parker, who had an eye for good-looking males, viewed Elvis in performance but focused less on the singer than on audiences' reaction to him. He realized the singer didn't need to limit himself to country and "hillbilly" music— he had potential in the wider musical spheres of recent "rock 'n roll" and timeless love ballads. Parker, a tireless promoter who'd developed several contacts over the years, moved in on Elvis' then-manager, eventually pushing him out of the picture.

But first, Parker had to win over Presley's parents, for Elvis was underage and couldn't sign his own contract. Vernon, who relished the idea of easy money, was quickly convinced. Gladys didn't trust the Colonel but after he sold Elvis' record contract with local Sun Records to RCA he acquired a devoted client for life. At first Parker took 25 percent of Presley's income (versus an agent's ten percent). Later 50 percent—and more, for Elvis didn't know about the Colonel's side deals. Nor did he realize why the greedy Parker routinely turned down myriad lucrative offers for Elvis to perform overseas. Parker didn't like to let his golden goose out of his sight. Not being a U.S. citizen and minus a passport, the Colonel couldn't have entered other countries nor been allowed back into the United States.

"Elvis Presley might be alive today if he'd [said yes to] the 1976 remake of *A Star Is Born*... Well before the 1969 demise of his screen acting career Elvis wanted and needed a hit. Barbra Streisand proposed co-starring [but] Kris Kristofferson later got the role and the film was a big hit.

Had Elvis co-starred... he'd have been a viable leading man again, made more films... and ended his total reliance on performing live. Once Tom Parker got proof that Elvis was a huge draw in Las Vegas and elsewhere—for, he'd flopped in Vegas in the '50s—he sent Elvis out on tour after tour.

The grueling pace, emotional demands and late hours (Elvis had long suffered from insomnia) fueled Presley's need for drugs. That was of less interest to his manager than the fact that the tours were under Parker's control, unlike films, where he'd had to contend with producers, directors and studio executives."

—From **Boze Hadleigh's** book
Scandals, Secrets & Swansongs
(EP may or may not have accepted
the actress-producer's offer, but if yes,
it was "the Colonel" who nixed it)

"Barbra has an eye for male beauty—look at her leading men. She and Elvis together would have sizzled... Due to the nature of his role, it would have been his sole chance for a possible Oscar nomination."

—**Natalie Wood**

"Elvis was truly an Adonis. But he didn't think himself handsome."

—Writer **Jess Stearn**

"He was the total androgynous beauty. I would practice Elvis in front of a mirror when I was 12 or 13 years old."
—Lesbian singer-songwriter **K.D. Lang**

"He's just a great big, beautiful hunk of forbidden fruit."
—A student of Mae Axton,
a teacher and early fan of EP

"From his hips to his lips to his tips on wowing the girls, the Presley boy is the genuine article."
—Columnist **Dorothy Kilgallen**

"In the 1950s Colonel Parker wasn't the only one who felt that Elvis, with his looks and crossover appeal, was wasted on country or hillbilly music… recording songs like 'Milkcow Blues Boogie.' Elvis went national after he plugged into rock 'n roll and ballads, you know, love songs."
—Co-star **Mary Tyler Moore**
(*Change of Habit*)

"The first time he went into Sun Studio it was still Memphis Recording Service. Elvis paid three bucks to record 'My Happiness' and 'That's When Your Heartaches Begin.' The record was a present to his mama… In a way, he had to get his mother out of his system before he could get loose enough for rock 'n roll."
—Singer **James Brown**

"Mr. Presley was a good ballad singer, but I believed he was talented and flexible enough to please Mr. Phillips [Sam Phillips, owner of Sun Records]. It took him a while to recognize what Elvis Presley had to offer."
—Sun office manager **Marion Keisker**

"Elvis was devastated when he tried out for the highly popular *Arthur Godfrey's Talent Scouts*. That program would have been a big national break for him, and he was slowly climbing the ladder. But Godfrey was tyrannical, jealous and petty. Elvis never got to meet him. Apparently, Godfrey's interviewer was under orders to meet Elvis, raise his hopes, then turn him down."

—TV talk host **Jack Paar**

"In May, 1954, Elvis auditioned to join the Stompers, which was Eddie Bond's band. Bond passed. Elvis later said Bond advised him to go back to driving a truck. Several people are supposed to have told him that."

—Lyricist **Howard Ashman**

"Sam Phillips was a businessman at heart. When he finally put in a call to Elvis Presley to record a song called 'Without You' he couldn't remember the name, called him 'the kid with the sideburns.' When the secretary called the Presley household Elvis reportedly ran all the way to the studio while she held the phone… His recording of the song was never released."

—*American Bandstand* host **Dick Clark**

"Elvis was far from an overnight sensation. He zigged and he zagged trying this, that and the other, here, there and everywhere in the South. It's just that when he hit, he hit so hard that suddenly everybody was aware of him… he appeared to have come out of nowhere.

"The North, the Midwest and the West didn't discover him until big-hit songs and, more importantly, television."

—Composer **Jay Livingston**

"The first name that later would stand alone was at first a liability. Many people I knew thought Elvis was pronounced El-viss, accent on the second syllable."

—Author **Helene Hanff**

"There's no definitive explanation of the name 'Elvis.' In Norse [Viking] mythology there is an Alvis... Elvis is related to Elwin... Eloise may be a female variant... The father's surname was originally spelled Pressley."

—Genealogist **Elbert (sic) Schnirdel**

"What he hated was the nickname Elvis the Pelvis. He considered it demeaning. In those days any reference to that portion of the anatomy was pretty bold or considered vulgar. Oddly, Elvis didn't like being reminded how sexual he was in public."

—Columnist **Shirley Eder**

"Elvis was nervous on stage when he did his first concert in 1954. One reason: he was the opening act for Slim Whitman, a big country music star... Elvis' legs shook while he performed, but it was rather endearing. You were *for* him... Soon he incorporated it into his performance, and the leg-shaking was sexy. It became a trademark."

—Singer/arranger **Kay Thompson**

"If Elvis would have had to stand and sing, stiff, like Sinatra, to name one, he'd have been more nervous. Because that wasn't him. What Elvis felt, he performed. He couldn't just stand there... he had to use his hands, his legs, his body... in fact his sexuality. He wasn't meant to fit a mold."

—**Paul Meehl**, clinical psychologist

"Once Presley realized the young audiences liked him being physically demonstrative he got lots more comfortable on stage… It also helped that the audiences were overwhelmingly young, so he didn't have a crowd of older disapproving faces glaring at him."

—Singer/songwriter **Del Shannon**

"Don't underestimate that lower lip! It was very full and very expressive. Elvis used it to full sexy advantage… He was very lucky not to have thin, chopped-liver lips."

—*Charro* co-star **Ina Balin**

"Elvis' lips naturally curled or curved to one side. It was a big part of his sexy image."

—Singer **Minnie Riperton**

"You look at that famous picture of Elvis and his parents when he was a toddler. The left side of his mouth was somewhat malformed. It corrected itself later, but not completely. Fortunately for him—and us!"

—Singer/songwriter **Peggy Lee**

"Elvis didn't smile, he sneered. Purposely? Or physiognomy? Whatever the cause, it turned most of the female public on."

—Radio host **Connie Norman**

"I'm sorry to say that until he became older and sort of a Vegas cartoon, a lot of males—singers and musicians and audience members—disliked Elvis Presley. There was plenty of jealousy."

—Musician **Doc Severinsen**

"Elvis Presley was the first masculine star since Rudolph Valentino in the 1920s to be widely criticized for being 'too sexy.' Men weren't supposed to be sex symbols, and weren't supposed to enjoy it."

—Author **Doug McClelland**

"In Lubbock, Texas, after a concert, a man in a car beckoned Elvis, who went over to him. The guy punched Elvis in the face and drove off."

—EP hairdresser **Larry Geller**

"When he got drafted and his career got suddenly interrupted, that brought him a lot of sympathy. Even guys sort of felt sorry for him. They could relate to the draft."

—Music journalist **Scott Timberg**

"Parents by the millions, particularly fathers, were glad the army sent for Elvis. They figured it would make a man of him and trim some of the hoochy-koochy sex symbol stuff off him."

—Actor **Richard Farnsworth**

"Elvis in the mid 1950s and Elvis in the mid 1960s were different public personas... Fifties Elvis was a threat, a musical and cultural revolutionary. Sixties Elvis was pasteurized, made acceptable and bland by Hollywood."

—Psychologist **Joyce Brothers**

"He was sort of torn. [During the '60s] Elvis loved all the money. But he missed all the song hits and live performing, the audience reaction... Hollywood and the Colonel used Elvis like a moneymaking machine.

But he went along with it—the more money, the better… quantity over quality."

—*Harum Scarum* co-star **Billy Barty**

"A blues singer named Arthur Crudup had recorded 'That's All Right, Mama' in the 1940s… That song has since been buried in the avalanche of subsequent Elvis song hits."

—Music historian **David O'Brien**

"What happened is, Elvis was basically performing country music, and even released records like 'Milkcow Blues Boogie.' But the growing teen audience pushed him into rock 'n roll. Country [music] was regional but rock 'n roll was growing nationally."

—Composer **Henry Mancini**

"When he went to Elvis' shows it was the crowd Parker watched, not Elvis."

—Writer **Alanna Nash**,
on future manager "Colonel" Tom Parker
sizing up the singer's effect on audiences

"Before Elvis, Tom Parker managed country singer Eddy Arnold. He helped him become a star in his field. But the Colonel was very controlling. He and Arnold quarreled once too often, so Arnold fired him. That gave Parker the motivation to go out and find some other singer to push and to make him as big a star as Eddy Arnold. Or bigger."

—**Maxene Andrews** of the Andrews Sisters

"I don't bad-mouth [Tom Parker]. But he'd be just as happy as a star in his own right as managing any star client."

—**Eddy Arnold** on his ex-manager

"Colonel Parker was looking for a talented boy singer... not a man singer. He wouldn't be able to manipulate or fool an average man as easily... Elvis Presley and Parker were made for each other, and it was lifelong."

—Singer/songwriter **Maurice Gibb** of the Bee Gees

"The Colonel was secretly going around inquiring if major record labels like RCA-Victor were willing to buy out Elvis Presley's contract with Sun Records. Elvis couldn't go national as a singer on a small label like Sun... He also got in good with Elvis' then-manager, Bob Neal, eventually and underhandedly taking over his position."

—Country singer **Slim Whitman**

"Colonel Parker knew he had to win over the folks, especially Gladys, to become Elvis' manager and steer his career. So he was already prepared when he met the parents... After he explained in detail the deals, the different media he planned to exploit, the profits to be made, Gladys's first question to the Colonel was which church did he attend?

She wanted to know he was a churchgoer... and not some Catholic or non-Christian. Naturally he supplied the answer that suited Gladys."

—Entourage member **Lamar Fike**

"Tom Parker made mega-millions off Elvis. That didn't prove he was a business whiz. He just happened to latch on to a goldmine. His background was carnivals. Some 15 years of third-rate traveling acts... One act he came up with was 'Colonel Parker's Dancing Chickens'—a hot plate sprinkled with sawdust that when he turned up the heat the baby chicks 'danced' for the customers."

—Theatre producer **Fritz Holt**

"He wasn't a colonel, he was Dutch, his real name was Andreas Cornelis [sic] van Kuijk. He was an illegal alien who smuggled himself into the United States in 1929... Ever wonder why Elvis never toured overseas although demand from London to Tokyo to Timbuktu was enormous? The Colonel wasn't a citizen, he had no passport—so he couldn't travel. Had the man ever left the USA, he wouldn't have been allowed back in."
—Journalist **Shana Alexander**

"Among the things the Colonel didn't do for his superstar client was create any tax shelters for Elvis. He was willing for Elvis to pay way in excess of what he might have owed the IRS, just to keep the Feds from investigating. The Colonel was terrified of receiving any personal attention from the U.S. government."
—Financial manager **Henry O'Neal**

"Colonel Tom Parker probably had another secret. Insiders guessed. Most denied... It didn't start to come out till after the Colonel died. Yes, he married. But women weren't his interest... and most of his assistants were good-looking young men."
—Columnist **Molly Ivins**

"What was the Colonel's sexual orientation? *Money*."
—**Martha Hyer**, wife of EP's
movie producer Hal Wallis

"What made Elvis Presley mainstream-friendly was movies. They watered him down. They were also the beginning of his end... formulaic because they were fiscally designed... and increasingly predictable. Movies changed radically in the '60s. But Elvis movies didn't. Why? The Colonel."

— Writer/producer **Marvin Jones**

"He starred in 31 movies, which ranged from mediocre to putrid, and just about in that order."

—Film critic **Pauline Kael**

"The Elvis Presley movies made television look good."

—TV producer **James Komack**

"You could well judge by the film titles. I mean, *Tickle Me, Girl Happy, Harum Scarum, Girls! Girls! Girls!* Same with the songs… 'Petunia, the Gardener's Daughter,' 'Clean Up Your Own Backyard,' 'Adam and Evil,' 'Long-Legged Girl'… need I say more? Could I say less?"

—Novelist **Jackie Collins**

"Between 1962 and 1969 the unthinkable happened: Elvis Presley had no number-one hit songs. In 1969 he quit acting in movies."

—Barry Manilow, American singer/songwriter

"I got seduced into a motion picture [*Just a Gigolo*, 1978] so ghastly it all but ruined me as an actor. It counts as my 31 Elvis films rolled into one."

—David Bowie

"The Colonel didn't know Elvis would last. He suspected Elvis was a fad. Most people thought rock 'n roll was a fad, it couldn't last longer than five, ten years. The Colonel marketed the hell out of Elvis while he was hot and selling all them records. Colonel did all the licensing, arranged it all. He wanted desperately to strike while that iron was still hot."

—*Girl Happy* co-star **Gary Crosby**

"Colonel Tom Parker gives capitalism a bad name. A total con man."

—Singer **Vic Damone**

"It's funny in a dismal way. I could say virtually anything I like about Elvis Presley's manager, without fear of reprisal. He wouldn't dare sue me, and many of us in show business know why."

—Songwriter and cabaret performer
Portia Nelson, alluding to Tom Parker's
illegal-alien status and fear of legal
and governmental processes

"I can't help thinking how much more of a man, or adult certainly, Eddy Arnold was than Elvis Presley. When Colonel Parker misbehaved one too many times Arnold fired him. Presley never had the guts."

—**Frank Sinatra Jr.**

"Someone should put in a good word for the Colonel. How much sooner might Elvis have started drugs if he hadn't had the Colonel at his elbow, ordering him to do this and not do that? The Colonel put the fear of God into Elvis. At least for a while."

—Newspaper editor **Rudy Kikel**

"The sad thing is, Colonel Parker didn't really think Elvis had much talent. Elvis' music wasn't Tom Parker's music. He was of another generation and he was Old World… waltzes and the like. But he knew his boy could draw crowds when he sang, and that's all that mattered to him."

—Pre-World War II "crooner" **Rudy Vallee**

"His first handful of movies had at least some merit. Some were dramatic, not yet that third-rate musical pap… He played an accidental killer who reforms in *Jailhouse Rock*… When Elvis and company realized that anything he appeared in made money they stopped caring about providing good entertainment. It became a sausage factory—just churn 'em out and collect the dough."

—Co-star **Charles Bronson** (*Kid Galahad*)

"I was in *Jailhouse Rock* with Presley, his third picture, I believe. He was still accessible, could act humble… he mixed with the cast and crew. As he should. I met him a few times years later. Didn't necessarily talk with him… always surrounded by his shock troops. I wonder how many of them graduated high school.

They were like gang members and he was their undisputed gang leader."

—Actor **Dean Jones**

"The part gives him scope to stop acting like an electrocuted baboon and to act like a human being, which he does with a new skill, a new restraint and a new charm."

—*New Chronicle* critic **Paul Dehn**
on EP in his fourth film, *King Creole*

"Elvis can act!"

—The *New York Times* on *King Creole*

"[*King Creole*] was his favorite of his own pictures. After completion of filming, he had ten days left to spend with his parents before going into the army... He wasn't going off to war, but Elvis thought he might never make another movie. He gave this performance all he had, without going overboard."
—Co-star **Walter Matthau**

"*King Creole*, yes. I directed the one and only believable Elvis Presley motion picture."
—Hungarian-born **Michael Curtiz**,
who helmed classics like
Casablanca and *Mildred Pierce*

"Elvis was off the big screen for almost two and a half years, a very long time in those days. From mid 1958 to late 1960. The comeback vehicle, to cash in on the army publicity, was *G.I. Blues*. Mediocre movie. So were most of what followed, until even die-hard fans got bored."
—*Coronet* magazine

"Elvis wanted nothing more to do with the army. But the Colonel shoved him into *G.I. Blues*. Commercially, it made sense. Artistically... what's that?"
—*Kid Galahad* co-star **Gig Young**

"We dated... *G.I. Blues* was clichéd, yet I enjoyed working with Elvis. He was so happy to be back working and out of the armed service... When someone told him I was from South Africa Elvis didn't believe it. He asked if both my parents were white. Yes... We had some good times. But he did say he did not want a working wife. Not working outside of his home."
—Leading lady **Juliet Prowse**

"I think his manager preferred surrounding Elvis with several females so no one actress could stand out... There were varying personal currents during shooting [of *Wild in the Country*, 1961]. I was the nominal leading lady but Elvis was clearly taken with teenage Tuesday Weld... Millie Perkins, I think, had a crush on Elvis, who flirted with all of us."

—**Hope Lange**

"Hope [Lange] was a nice lady but she did imbibe. She liked vodka, and Presley, who was new to vodka, joined right in with her. Not just once or twice. Later I heard that was about the time he started allowing his Memphis buddies to bring liquor into his house."

—Co-star **Gary Lockwood**

"It was about control and bad taste—his manager's. For example, Elvis could have co-starred in a music-free picture with Robert Mitchum, reportedly one of his favorites. Guess who turned it down?... After Elvis made his first million, thus 'a millionaire,' he felt forever beholden to the man he thought was Midas."

—Screenwriter **Jay Presson Allen**

"Elvis blamed his poor Hollywood rep on Hollywood. Nope. It was him and the Colonel, traveling the path of least resistance."

—*Buzz* editor **Donald Rawley**

"Of course, we never worked together. But for an excruciating number of films Elvis Presley and I were under contract to Hal B. Wallis. That man helped produce some of the best pictures ever made while he was at Warners. Then, as an independent producer, it was good, bad or in between—just so long as it turned a nifty profit."

—**Shirley MacLaine**

"For *Fun in Acapulco* there were publicity photos taken of Elvis in a lifeguard's bathing suit. He was held up horizontally by several young men. Like a surfboard. When the photographer was finished, Elvis looked pale and… startled.

"His manager asked what was wrong. Elvis said one of the men holding him up had squeezed, you know, his man part. The manager laughed. But Elvis was angry and told him never again to hire another man like that."

—Co-star **Ursula Andress**

"In *Fun in Acapulco* our characters were unfriendly rivals. It spilled a little into our off-camera relationship. He was never rude but… for one thing, he wasn't the only actor on the set that women found attractive. I don't think he was used to that."

—**Alejandro Rey**

"What limited his products' appeal was the lack of exciting leading ladies, real stars. Of course he always had to end up with an actress, but those cast were of no real interest and their roles were one-dimensional. Ann-Margret was the lone exception."

—Producer **Renee Valente**

"It was all over town… The Colonel battled MGM, the director [of *Viva Las Vegas*], the publicists… everyone but Ann-Margret herself. They were building her up, giving her close-ups, praising her star quality… Parker was furious, kept yelling it was supposed to be an Elvis Presley picture! He didn't want 'the girl' interfering or taking away from Elvis.

"And when it was a bigger hit than usual he was still furious… and didn't let a female 'compete' with Elvis again."

—Paramount executive **A.C. Lyles**

"Colonel Parker with his cheesy old-fashioned ideas was a total male chauvinist pig. Had no use for women. Every movie needed one, but beyond that…"

—Co-star **Sheree North** (*The Trouble with Girls (And How to Get Into It)*)

"Priscilla was waiting in the wings, but Elvis wasn't inclined to restrict himself… He did consider Ann-Margret for a wife. If she gave up her career. Fortunately, she went on to a longer and more distinguished film career than he had."

—Screenwriter and AMPAS president **Fay Kanin**

"Countless starlets in his movies. Like disposable candy… a former Miss America [Mary Ann Mobley], Christina Crawford, the Batgirl [Yvonne Craig] from TV's *Batman* to Ellie Mae [Donna Douglas] from *The Beverly Hillbillies* and Nancy Sinatra. They and the too many movies were too interchangeable."

—Cinematographer **Néstor Almendros**

"If it had been publicized later, I'd've had to live it down… but I was in an Elvis Presley flick. At least I played a judge."

—Two-time Oscar winner **Jason Robards Jr.**

"I resented the way veteran actors, actresses, anyone in front of the camera, was made to feel it was darn special to be in 'an Elvis Presley.' All of us veteran actors had been in far better pictures… this was frankly what some of us were reduced to."
—Co-star **Burgess Meredith** (*Stay Away Joe*)

"I knew he was trying to impress me and I didn't cotton to it. He knew my work—I'd been around a long time… The picture, *Kid Galahad* [1962], about a fighter, was a for-the-money remake of a '30s movie with Bogart in it. This one was Elvis the singing boxer. I played his trainer. He tried to play a boxer… Good thing his reputation rests on his music, not his pictures."
—**Charles Bronson**

"The impression Elvis gave some movie-union people was he was above the rules. Specifically, hair. Those people's job is styling, coloring and cutting a star's hair according to the character he portrays… [but] Presley would typically breeze into the studio with a personal barber and get his usual haircut, his hair already dyed black-black, which grew monotonous."
—Philanthropist **Sybil Brand**,
widow of Fox publicist Harry Brand

"Words and Elvis didn't agree. His forte was lyrics. Singing, he was magical. Talking —or talkin'—he was… I'll say it: kinda dumb."
—*Girl Happy* co-star **Gary Crosby**

"Elvis worked with a few real stars like Barbara Stanwyck, Dolores Del Rio and Lizabeth Scott. But they were older and played bosses or relatives. I was a star too, but long ago; I gave up that goldfish bowl. I liked working with Elvis but those scripts! Whoo—they stank.

Everyone makes a stinker now and then. But one after another?"

—Joan Blondell (*Stay Away Joe*)

"When Barbra Streisand and Elvis met in Las Vegas and she asked him to co-star in *A Star Is Born* he was very intrigued by her long fingernails and held her fingers. To show how the press can exaggerate, some accounts reported that Presley dropped to one knee and started painting Barbra's fingernails."

—Author **Paul Rosenfield**

"Elvis Presley would have been a better male lead in Barbra Streisand's *A Star Is Born* than Kris Kristofferson. Barbs and Elvis would have shot sparks off each other... a historic teaming... I heard the Colonel wanted too big of a hunk of the recording profits and I've heard Elvis was fascinated by Streisand but intimidated by her."

—Actor **Ron Vawter**

"Elvis knew Streisand's movies were money-spinners. He seemed willing to take second billing and was said to relish the idea of playing an out-of-control rock star... It may be that Tom Parker emphasized that the role offered Presley was a washed-up star and addict who dies at the end. Her part was the rising star, the survivor.

"Maybe they both feared she'd overwhelm him or make him a supporting character—she was producing the movie."

—Film publicist **Ed Margulies**

"Say what you will about his movies, but while he was laboring in film after film there was discipline... enforced. The studios made him toe the line. After Elvis left that system and labored in concert after concert, no one kept him in line. His behavior and habits went downhill."

—Musicologist **Alan Lomax**

"It was the early '70s, I think in Detroit, when Red [West] discovered a cocaine package that arrived for Elvis through a singer in the group. Red confronted the singer, violently, warned him about being a supplier... Elvis heard about it, told Red he didn't like 'bully tactics' and said he *needed* the cocaine.

Red was appalled but knew it was useless to argue. Elvis had often made it clear, 'If you don't like my behavior, there's the fucking door.'"

—Cousin **Billy Smith**

"I'm backstage waiting for Elvis to arrive. He pulls up in the car, and he fell out of the limousine, to his knees. People jumped to help, and he pushed them away like, 'Don't help me.' He walked onstage and held on to the mic for the first 30 minutes like it was a post.

Everybody's looking at each other like, Is the tour gonna happen? Is he sick? Is it gonna be canceled?"

—Keyboardist **Tony Brown**

"I worked with Elvis early on, and I just have to smile. Because big ole fame, Elvis-size fame, can really twist your ego... We heard how some kin of Elvis was complainin' about the rain one night, wishing it would finally stop. So Elvis, y'see, he says, 'No problem, I'll take care of it.' And he holds his hands up to the sky and, lo and behold, that rain just stops.

"And you know somethin'? By that time, I think ole Elvis really did feel that he had a personal connection up with heaven itself."

—**Andy Griffith**

"Colonel Parker kept Elvis aloof from other people, the better to control him. He wouldn't let Elvis give interviews or do benefits. Elvis did not attend movie premieres nor do publicity to promote his pictures.

The official excuses were Elvis' shyness and the crowd-control problem—neither of which stopped other big or bigger movie stars."

—*Kid Galahad* co-star **Gig Young**

"I have to say this because one of his co-stars [Mary Tyler Moore] repeatedly says she was the only leading lady Elvis Presley did not sleep with. I know of other actresses besides myself who didn't sleep with Elvis Presley. Including Miss Dolores Hart, who made two pictures with him before she stopped acting to become a nun."

—Swiss actress **Ursula Andress**, the first "Bond Girl"

"If you want the truth, Presley didn't have friends. He had employees, his Memphis mafia. They were on-call 24 hours a day, most every day of the year, a paid entourage of six or seven young men who provided paid companionship, security and did Elvis' bidding."

—**Norman Taurog**, who directed EP in several movies

"Unlike other stars or more urbane and knowledgeable types, the Memphis mafia were never a threat to Tom Parker's hold on Elvis. They were partly designed to keep outsiders away."

—*Interview* editor **Ingrid Sischy**

"Those guys, his Memphis mafia, might as well have been robots. There was nothing there. No interaction, no real thought process. Certainly no advising Elvis or standing up to him. Ever."

—Co-star **Burgess Meredith**

"The Colonel wanted to be the sole influence on Elvis outside his immediate family... Probably the friend Parker hated the most was Larry Geller. Elvis thought he was smart and consulted him on spiritual matters.

When Larry was growing a beard the Colonel saw another chance to demean him. Parker hated beards. Anyhow he convinced Elvis to tell Geller the beard was embarrassing to their movie producer Hal Wallis."

— EP's stepbrother **Rick Stanley**

"Hal would sometimes say life would be so much easier without [Parker's] interference. He said money, meddling and making mountains out of molehills were the man's chief joys."

—Actress **Martha Hyer**, movie producer
Hal Wallis' second wife

"It's sad and not very flattering to Elvis, but where he used to defend Geller against the Colonel, finally he stopped. The Colonel wore Elvis down... Elvis resented the Colonel in several ways and with good reason, but he shied away from having to confront the old bastard."

—Entourage member **Lamar Fike**

"Most of the time the 'mafia' led a life that took on the appearance of a young boy's fantasies. They would ride motorcycles in packs, calling themselves El's Angels, clown around, play football and hold open house parties on weekends.

There was an endless supply of girls, mostly in their teens and early twenties. Elvis lived like a rajah, surrounded by an ever-changing harem of admiring females."

—From *Elvis: The Films and Career of Elvis Presley*

"It was weird. We'd sit around watching television— that's what we did 75 percent of the time—and nobody'd ever laugh at anything unless Elvis did. If Elvis laughed, everybody'd just roar. Not more than Elvis laughed, but just as much."

—Female visitor at Graceland, quoted by EP biographer Boris Zmijewsky

"The Memphis mafia would do anything to hang on to their jobs, and Elvis knew it. More than once he got so mad that he fired them—each and every one. They would pack their bags and depart Graceland. Then, when they reached the airport and were feeling their worst, Elvis would call and inform them he'd changed his mind, that they had their jobs back, but to hurry on back as quick as possible."

—Singer **Susannah McCorkle**

"Sylvester Stallone once explained that some stars treat others badly because of all the shit they had to put up with, climbing the ladder. That's a crappy excuse, but it may explain why Elvis Presley turned out the way he did, especially during the 1970s, his final and uncompleted decade."

—Celebrity photographer **E.L. Woody**

"Elvis was fun, a star-struck kid when I knew him. He liked to perform for you. Good manners. He wanted to impress and he loved meeting celebrities… he wanted so much to join the group. However, movie stardom apparently grew his ego and shrank his world… He went into the next thing to seclusion."

—Pianist and singer **Liberace**

In the mid 1950s "Elvis thought I was a big star. We hung out together and he'd talk about his hopes and dreams. He asked questions about how I handled different situations and about the fans, my life at home. It was very flattering. I knew already he was going to be a bigger star than I ever would be."

—Actor **Nick Adams**

"In 1956 the media was full of Elvis 'dating' Natalie Wood, who was in *Rebel Without a Cause* the year before. But it wasn't that… Nick Adams, who was in *Rebel*, introduced her to Elvis, and Nick and Natalie and a bunch of friends went around with Elvis for a while… I think Elvis' manager broke it up. He wanted Elvis to be a celebrity *apart*."

—**Ervin Roeder**, Nick Adams' friend and attorney

"Robert Wagner did indeed declare that Natalie never dated Elvis Presley. For image reasons I can't legally go into, Wagner wanted to seem like the only man in her life."

—Director **Stanley Donen**, who was married
to Wagner's second wife

"I think the friendship with Nick Adams ended after there were underground rumors about it… Nick was gay or supposedly bi. Either Elvis or Colonel Tom Parker broke it up. Nick certainly didn't."

—Adams's co-star **Rock Hudson**

"Elvis was so impressed by my mom getting me started in show business… He'd seen most of my movies. *Rebel Without a Cause* was his favorite. He couldn't believe I got an Oscar nomination for it—which was a compliment, though.

When I knew Elvis, he was spontaneous and very open. Unlike Jimmy, who was closed off and sort of calculating. People said Elvis changed a lot, later on."

—**Sal Mineo**

"It's somewhat amusing that early on, Elvis Presley was friends with Liberace, Nick Adams, Sal Mineo, Sammy Davis Jr., various gay and bisexual men. I doubt Elvis was aware of it. Maybe he thought everybody was drawn to him… I do hope he let them down easy."

—Hollywood publicist **Patty Freedman**

"Presley made a study of popular male stars. He did his homework. In the end it didn't pay off. Once he hit pay dirt he was afraid to try anything different. So he repeated himself into celluloid jokedom."

—**Burt Reynolds**

"When I played Conrad Birdie on Broadway, I wasn't imitating Elvis Presley… and I was told to deny it was about Elvis. *Bye Bye Birdie* was about a songwriter and a female fan who come into contact with Conrad before he's drafted into the army."

—**Dick Gautier**

"Somebody said one of the producers was contacted by the famous Colonel Parker when *Bye Bye Birdie* was first announced. Primarily he wanted to know if anyone in Elvis' circle was going to be in it. Like primarily a character based on Parker. They said he was pretty worried.

Then, when he contacted the studio about the film version, the studio told cast and crew, everyone, to ignore any and all communication from the Colonel and just move forward."

—**Jesse Pearson**, who played
Conrad Birdie on screen

"I was never told to be or to approximate Elvis. I think for legal safety. I was told to 'think Elvis.' Which to me that meant think sexy. So I did!… *Bye Bye Birdie* was a solid hit, though it didn't do that much for me or the girl who got replaced in the [1963] movie by Ann-Margret.

A long time later there was a Broadway sequel, *Bring Back Birdie*. A big, big flop. Its time had passed, like with Elvis."

—**Dick Gautier**

"I don't know why they kept some of the Broadway actors, like Dick Van Dyke and Paul Lynde and let others go. But I was thrilled to be in the movie… My two songs were firecrackers and the whole score was terrific. It was a bang-up success and everyone loved it. I heard Elvis liked it too—he also liked Ann-Margret."

—Actor **Jesse Pearson**

"*Bye Bye Birdie* was put together carefully... every song had a strong melody and good lyrics. Its casting included several talents... Ironically and definitely it was better than anything poor Elvis Presley appeared in. As a sensational star, he deserved better."

—**Maureen Stapleton**,
who appeared in the film version

"You could enjoy *Bye Bye Birdie* without knowing Birdie was Elvis... Decades after seeing it I was informed it's also based on Conway Twitty. *Who?* I thought that name was a cartoon character, like Tweety Bird. Seems the backers were afraid of Colonel Parker, so they named the character Conrad Birdie to sound more like Conway Twitty, who I think is a country singer."

—Theatre producer **Lore Noto**

"Today Elvis is popular despite his movies... thanks to his music and his Look. And Graceland, the most popular private residence open to the paying public in the entire USA."

—Cable talk show host **Skip E. Lowe**

"Hard to believe, but some years after he broke through in 1955 a lot of people and the media wondered if the Elvis fad would soon be over. I remember headlines like 'Will Presley's Appeal Last?' and 'Elvis: How Much Longer?' What extended his fame was the movies.

Think, how enduringly famous would Crosby, Doris Day, Sinatra or Streisand be if they hadn't made movies? You can face-lift an actor, but you can't rejuvenate a singer's ageing voice."

—Talent manager **Brad Grey**

"What soiled Elvis' image was those movies and then those Vegas costumes. I like the original, pure Elvis—the pre-Hollywood, pre-pills singer… He died young-ish but if he'd died even younger, before going Hollywood, I think he'd be as big or bigger than he is today, and minus the jokes, the tackiness and all the negatives."

—**Russell King**, *New York Times* deputy news editor

"His manager told a screenwriter friend of mine there were half a million hard-core fans who would go out to see every Elvis picture three times or more. Virtually every year there were three new Elvis pictures… The Colonel would tell associates that those fans' taste was 100 percent Elvis and they would go see anything at all he appeared in. The Colonel was quite proud and happy about that!"

—Movie producer **Hal B. Wallis**

"What I had against Parker was that he was a tasteless man who had power and used it."

—**Philip Dunne**, director of EP's
Wild in the Country

"Elvis wouldn't stand up for himself because the Colonel was a great businessman. No one in Elvis' family had a head for business, and he was afraid of making a wrong move—it was torture for him."

—**Red West**, who worked on 27 EP movies

"Uncanny. The man's influence over Elvis Presley… a strange, hypnotic, almost total control over Elvis."

—Producer/director **Steve Binder**

"People used to say Colonel Parker was Presley's Svengali. That story was super-famous, everyone knew what it meant. But you didn't see it in print much because the singer that Svengali controlled was a female," named Trilby.

—Co-star **Glenda Farrell** (*Kissin' Cousins*)

"Colonel Parker said, 'Are you the boy who wrote that [song] "Little Less Conversation"?' I said yes. He said, 'You a pretty good-lookin' boy, you're going to be a star.' I said, 'Well, thank you very much.'
He said, 'You want the Colonel to rub your head?'

I'm looking around… but these guys with him are dead serious, they're all just looking at me. So, I bent over, and he put his hand on my head, like Oral Roberts, and he said, 'You're going to be a star. You tell everybody the Colonel touched your head.'"

—Songwriter turned singer **Mac Davis**

"Elvis had two fathers—Vern and the Colonel. And after Gladys was gone, Colonel Parker was father and mother… and jailer—or would-be jailer. He seemed to want sole possession."

—Army buddy and friend **Rex Mansfield**

"No contest: the Colonel had much more say in Elvis' life than his father did."

—Co-star and girlfriend **Juliet Prowse**

"Tom Parker was a details man. He loved arranging things, planning, scheming, bargaining… coming out on top. Neither Elvis nor his dad had a head for numbers, and details escaped Elvis and bored him. Compared to them, Parker was a genius."

—EP biographer **Albert Goldman**

"His apologists will say that though the Colonel helped himself, and how, he also helped Elvis Presley become such a big star. But Elvis would still have become a big star without the Colonel. Maybe a little later… Happily, the Colonel is almost forgotten, while Elvis is not."

—Singer **George Michael**

"Every motion picture Elvis was in had a credit: 'Technical Advisor—Colonel Tom Parker.' A farce… what did he advise? He knew zilch about moviemaking."

—Director **George Sidney** (*Viva Las Vegas*)

"A lot of people in America looked up to Elvis Presley… an icon, a success. They didn't in Hollywood. People here knew he was just a shallow puppet, willing to do anything his boss told him to do."

—Movie distribution executive **Harry Walders**

"Elvis often complained about the movies 'they' put him in, like he had no say in the matter. You can't name one other movie star who was so hands-off about his own screen career or so manipulated. Nobody could understand it… but there were plenty of theories!"

—Professor of media psychology **Stuart Fischoff**

"There were outlandish 'explanations' for the Colonel's grip on Elvis. Two of the wildest... that fat old Tom had some kind of sexual hold on Elvis. I can't imagine anybody having anything sexual to do with that fella. Including his apparently platonic wife, who was older than him.

The other was also false but more plausible: that Elvis was mixed-race—he did come from the South—and the Colonel kept it secret so long as Elvis handed him that big portion of his income and followed orders."

—Actor/singer **Jim Nabors**, an Alabama native best known for his role as Gomer Pyle

"One of those scandal-type magazines insinuated that Elvis might be gay... mostly based on his being so overtly sexy and then staying single for so long. But he wasn't. Alas."

—Gay UK photo archivist **Gil Gibson**

"Colonel Tom was smart... he surrounded Elvis with praise. He pulled all the strings himself, did all the negotiating, all the hard stuff, including the publicity. The only stress on Elvis was to get up and perform and hear the applause. Elvis was insulated from the real world.

Colonel Tom played the money and loyalty buttons, helping form or reshape the Memphis mafia, which was Elvis' security blanket and his serfs. Colonel Tom ruled Elvis. But Elvis ruled his little kingdom of well-paid cronies."

—**Henry McClurg**, newspaper publisher

"Nothing was too demeaning for those 'mafia' boys. Like if Elvis went to the john he'd clean up after himself but then he'd stand there, bare-assed, shout out a name, and that guy would come rushing through the door. 'The pants, man, the pants.' The guy would sink to his knees and start pulling up Elvis' tight pants for him—and Elvis didn't always wear underwear."

—**Joe Esposito**, EP's road manager

"Part of the Colonel's strategy was to keep Elvis happy and distracted. To keep him out of his hair, financially, and keep him from asking questions—which he wouldn't know what to ask, anyway. Had he needed to, Parker would have acted as Elvis' pimp, to keep him otherwise engaged. But that's one service Elvis never required."

—Composer/lyricist **Michael Friedman**

"Colonel Parker was fundamentally two things—a publicist and a negotiator. And a third thing people, including Elvis, didn't know about—a con man who made deals on the side for himself. Some only came to light after Elvis died."

—Singer and co-star **Barbara McNair**
(*Change of Habit*)

"Parker could have let Elvis alternate performing live, which was his true love, and making fewer and better pictures. But whenever money could be made quicker and bigger, that was the Colonel's choice and Elvis went along… Neither had a long-range vision."

—Co-star **Sterling Holloway**
(*Live a Little, Love a Little*)

"When Elvis' movies were floundering the first thing the Colonel could think of was to double his managerial fee to 50 percent. So he wouldn't experience a big dip in his income. This was not a manager who put his client's best interests first."

—Novelist **Jackie Collins**

"Tom Parker had no shame and gall to spare. Asking Elvis Presley for half his income. What truly astounds is that Elvis Presley gave it to him."

—Publicist **Andrea Jaffe**

"Parker became a gambling addict. That became a headache for Elvis when the man actually asked him for more money… also an embarrassment because knowledge about Parker's huge losses was becoming public knowledge."

—Las Vegas comedian **Shecky Green**

"The Colonel never stopped hustling. One reason, his mounting gambling debts… As late as 1974 he devised Boxcar Productions, a company to promote Elvis products. He benefited the most, got 40 percent, while four other guys, including Elvis Presley, divided the remaining 60 percent—15 percent each.

"I wouldn't doubt the Colonel explained it to Elvis something like, 'You see, I don't get 50 percent— nowhere near that, son.' Unbelievable."

—**Charles Aidikoff**, operator of a chain
of screening rooms

"Colonel Parker hypocritically laid down the law for Presley. But he wouldn't control his own gambling, which is also an addiction… A friend told me that when a gambler keeps losing, that's when he doesn't think about stopping. That's what happened with Parker. He lost most of everything he ever earned or finagled."

—Columnist **Radie Harris**

"I wouldn't doubt that Parker didn't mind terribly about Elvis becoming a drug addict. Wouldn't that make him easier to control?"

—**Dick Gautier**

"While Elvis was getting fat and deeper into drugs, his supposed mentor and lifelong manager was looking ahead to how he could increase and prolong his own earnings. His behavior was criminal."

—**Frank Sinatra Jr.**

"The Colonel assumed Elvis would outlive him. He didn't mind selling off pieces of Elvis for exorbitant sums of cash... Unbelievably, he sold off the royalties to Elvis' songs and records!... The Colonel had sometimes coerced the songs' composers into adding or substituting Elvis' name as a co-writer or composer."

—Business advisor **Lane S. Pincus**

"Even after the death of his single client, Parker's management contract—which Vernon Presley renewed on the day of his son's funeral—continued to give him 50 percent of the income from Elvis' estate. After a labyrinthine number of injunctions and hearings, Elvis Presley Enterprises was able, in 1983, to depose Parker—especially after courts took a close look at his shady commercial-licensing deals, his failure to retain Elvis' record royalties and his status as an illegal alien who never pursued U.S. citizenship.

It didn't come cheap. Parker reportedly received a two-million-dollar payoff, and in 1990 EPE paid him much more for his private collection of Elvis memorabilia—some 70,000 pounds of scrapbooks, photos, Elvis fan club archives, unseen video footage, clothes (including Elvis' gold lamé suit) and other stuff currently cached in a Memphis warehouse" as of 1999.

—From *Elvis Culture: Fans, Faith & Image*

"It was Elvis' mother Gladys who never fully trusted Parker. She said he seemed a shifty character. Little did she know...."

—Entourage member **Marty Lacker**

"Elvis liked me, and I liked him. He had no jealousy toward me... in fact he would repeat how much he enjoyed my series [*My Favorite Martian*]. We worked together more than once... There is no doubt in my mind that Elvis Presley would have lived longer had he never met Tom Parker or whatever his real name was."

—**Bill Bixby**

"How ironic that it was TV that resurrected Elvis' career after he became a virtual has-been in movies. It shows how low the Colonel had sunk, after years of looking down his stubby nose at television. But it was that 1968 NBC-TV special that turned things around for Elvis Presley."

—Actor **Dick Van Patten**

"If the1968 TV special had been akin to the Elvis motion pictures, the industry would have concluded he could no longer cut it on the big screen or little screen.

But for once Tom Parker's bad taste and pandering to convention didn't carry the day, and Elvis did it his way."

—Actor **William Schallert**,
Screen Actors Guild president

"The Colonel stepped in when Elvis' movie career was shot. Less to improve things than to try and make them more money. He induced NBC to finance a TV special plus another movie. No one would pay Elvis top-dollar any more, so this was the best deal available. But the Colonel wanted Elvis to open the special with 'Good evening, ladies and gentlemen,' sing a few dozen Christmas songs, then close with 'Merry Christmas and good night.'

Steve Binder, the director, wanted a hipper Elvis who acknowledged his rock 'n roll roots… and instead of a suit, black leather. A sexy, exciting Elvis, not the faded figure the Colonel preferred. Elvis sided with the younger director against 'the old man.'"

—Actor and co-star **Gary Crosby**
(son of singer Bing Crosby)

"After [the taping] was all over, Elvis asked me what I thought as far as the future was concerned? I said, 'Elvis, my real feeling is I don't know if you'll do any great things you want to do. Maybe the bed has been made already, maybe this'll be just a little fresh air you'll experience for a month. Maybe you'll go back to making another 25 of those movies.'

He said, 'No, no, I won't. I'm going to do things now!'"

—TV director **Steve Binder**

"In Europe the rumor persists that Andreas Cornelis van Kuijk murdered a woman in 1929 and that is why he fled to the United States within several hours on a ship. To judge by the ruthlessness and mendacity of the man once he reached American shores, it is not impossible to believe."

—Spanish writer **Juan Goytisolo**

"Whatever desperate act caused Andeas van Kuijk, later known as Tom Parker, to escape with basically just the clothes on his back, we shall never know, thanks to the Nazis… their bombing of the Netherlands during World War II and the loss of so many files and records, including criminal records."

—Dutch actor **Willem van Stratten**

PART THREE:
ENDURING STARDOM

Enduring Stardom

Inevitably, the handsome, sexy singer transferred to the silver screen, where he was first-billed in all his movies after the first one—which was retitled *Love Me Tender* after a song Elvis sang in it. His early vehicles varied in quality but were all hits. Then the U.S. Army beckoned and Presley believed his booming singing and film careers were over. But the wily Colonel kept Elvis' name in the news during his years stationed in Germany. He'd had Elvis record extra songs, to release during his well-publicized absence, and when Elvis returned he was starred, reluctantly, in a movie called *G.I. Blues*. Unpublicized was the fact of Elvis, 24, dating a 14-year-old who was being groomed as a possible future wife.

During the 1960s Elvis' song hits ceased, not only because of the Beatles and other newcomers but because Tom Parker had discovered that mediocre songs didn't detract from Presley pictures' popularity. To gain extra royalties the Colonel insisted songwriters relinquish their copyrights and/or add Elvis' name as co-writer; naturally, first-rank songwriters refused. Parker also declined worthwhile celluloid projects for his client that veered from the easy, proven formula and offered "competition" in the form of name co-stars of either gender. The Colonel preferred Elvis to appear opposite starlets than major actresses and was incensed when MGM treated Ann-Margret as an equal co-star in *Viva Las Vegas*—which became Presley's most popular movie. The too-frequent Elvis films were shot more and more quickly and kept repeating themselves until even fans got bored... the Colonel, with Presley's consent, had run Elvis' screen career into the ground.

Parker, who didn't like Elvis to do charity or free concerts—he'd declined the Army's requests for Private Presley to sing to the troops—and who looked down on television, in desperation arranged a TV special for his sole client. Not having performed live for several years, a nervous Elvis feared ridicule and low ratings. But his 1968 TV comeback, influenced more by its hip young director than the old-fashioned Colonel, inspired the return of Elvis as a top-draw live performer. Though he'd flopped in Las Vegas in the 1950s, Elvis Presley became an ongoing institution there in the '70s. He began years of touring the country, to the delight of a manager who could exercise far more control over concert performances than motion pictures which involved studios, executives and directors.

"He was close to crying… he asked, 'Do you realize I'll never know if a woman loves me or Elvis Presley?'"
—Hairdresser and "spiritual advisor" **Larry Geller**

"Everyone under a certain age has forgotten what a furor Elvis caused… denounced in pulpits, magazines, newscasts… there were calls for boycotts… Seems anything new, anyone sexy or different, from Marilyn Monroe to the Beatles, causes such an indignant reaction, particularly in the States."
—British singer **Dusty Springfield**

"The media covered rising star Elvis Presley more like a freak or a social problem than a new talent or a new personality. I think that left a mark on him, made him insecure… it made him more of a loner."
—Author and professor **Carolyn G. Heilbrun**

"It hurt Elvis how many of the people he admired in show business cold-shouldered him. It took years for the controversy around him to wear off… but then he in turn cold-shouldered 'controversial' newcomers."
—**Freddie Mercury**

"In Las Vegas I was nearby when Cary Grant, who I think had a crush on Elvis, came up after the show. They cleared the way for him and he went right to Elvis and told him he was the greatest entertainer since Jolson. There was this silence, whether from embarrassment or ignorance… I half expected Elvis to say Jolson-who?"
—EP fan **Sheila Metcalf**

"Before he became reclusive, socializing only with no-brains-required Memphis mafia, Elvis enjoyed meeting and having his picture taken with big celebrities... Once he became a big celebrity, his insecurity surfaced. Most were more educated, more articulate, had more to say... He avoided comparisons and competition, retreating into his dark little Elvis world. And I mean dark—the man didn't like sunlight!"

—**Joan Rivers**, who tried in vain
to interview EP

"Did you ever see Elvis on a talk show? Just as well. To keep the mystique, keep the boob off the tube."

—Comedian **Sam Kinison**

"Elvis once participated in a late-night jam session that also counted Jerry Lee Lewis. But he steered clear of him... he felt Lewis was self-destructive and an example to avoid. Elvis didn't like associating with people he thought were crazy or unsuccessful."

—Uncle **Vester Presley**

"In 1976 Jerry Lee Lewis was arrested in the wee hours of the morning in front of Graceland's gates. 'The Killer,' as Lewis called himself, was drunk, disorderly and armed with a .38 derringer. 'I was really rockin' that night,' he would later laugh."

—*Life* Magazine

"I never felt myself in competition with anyone. I was just amazed any of it happened to me. But more than a few insiders told me Elvis Presley admired me and was jealous of me. I was a millionaire by 21 and for a time I got more fan mail than he did, although who was counting all those letters I couldn't say."

—Teen heartthrob **Ricky Nelson**

"Elvis told me how much he liked my act and admired my talent... he said he wished he could play the piano like I did. I said I liked him too."

—**Liberace**

"Time changes our view and perspective of things. When Elvis recorded one of his now-classics, 'Blue Suede Shoes,' Carl Perkins had recently recorded it. Perkins was far more respected than Elvis and his version of the song far out-sold Elvis'. But today not many people remember Carl Perkins."

—**Neil Bogart**, founder of Casablanca Records

"When we were readying for his second picture Elvis came to me and asked if he had to smile in it. I asked why? He said he'd been studying actors he admired, like Bogart, Brando and James Dean. He said they never smiled.

I said I never thought of that. Elvis said, 'Everybody smiles except the people you remember.'"

—Writer-director **Hal Kanter** (*Loving You*)

"Elvis said his goal was to become a movie star who lasted."

—Paramount executive **A.C. Lyles**

"Paramount secured Elvis Presley, to the chagrin of Ed Muhl, VP in charge of production at Universal. You've seen his name at the front of dozens of Universal pictures but probably not noticed it. Ed, who was 'gay closet,'

Boze Hadleigh

1950s, was dying to sign Elvis but didn't dare push too hard… I believe he undertook secret negotiations but the Presley manager was too greedy or some perks were withheld—not by Ed Muhl, by the others at Universal."

—film director **George Cukor**

"A prime reason Universal didn't sign Elvis was they had big, handsome Rock Hudson. Rock wasn't a major talent, although more so than Elvis…

He did get one Academy Award nomination. Elvis and Oscar were utter strangers.

Rock got to do better pictures than Elvis, including *Giant* [1956]. Though I could picture Elvis in the role James Dean did in *Giant*. But no doubt the Colonel would have quashed it. He didn't care about Elvis becoming a star actor. He just wanted a profitable star."

—Writer/producer **Marvin Jones**

"He once confided that one of his biggest regrets was his mama didn't live long enough so he could take her to see each and every one of his movies, just the two of them eating popcorn and hot dogs together, watching Elvis."

—Actor **Nick Adams**

"Elvis had a typed-out list of things his screen characters would never do. It was only three things— the second was redundant at the time. One, his characters would not do drugs. Two, they wouldn't remove their pants without underwear. Three, and I remember this verbatim, an Elvis character would 'not be unmanly and let some girl dominate him.'"

—**Martha Hyer**, widow of producer Hal Wallis, who signed EP to a movie contract

"Not so smart, that wheeler-dealer Colonel. He signed Presley to producer Hal Wallis for $100,000 a picture. The Colonel and Elvis thought this was fantastic. It was—for a first picture. But the contract had an option for six more pictures, each at the same price. No matter how successful. Long-term, it was a stupid move."

—Producer/director **Billy Wilder**

"It's difficult to be certain without seeing actual documents. Some sources say Parker out-negotiated Hal Wallis, some say he could have done better. He did very well for a Southern boy who came up from poverty and for himself, needless to say. But Colonel Parker's deals weren't record-breakers except years after, for live performances."

—Film critic **Gene Siskel**

"It's also about percentages, completion dates, etc. Elizabeth Taylor was the first star to earn a million for one movie [*Cleopatra*, 1963]. Due to overtime and other clauses, she earned much more than that for it... Elvis Presley had to do about three pictures a year to make what someone like [Clark] Gable did with one picture a year."

—Critic and film writer **Wyatt Cooper** (Anderson's father)

"I felt the same thrill I experienced when I first saw Errol Flynn on the screen. Elvis, in a very different, modern way, had exactly the same power, virility and sexual drive. The camera caressed him."

-–**Hal B. Wallis**, on EP's screen test

"The writing was on the wall when Elvis' first film, a Civil War story, had its title changed from *The Reno Brothers* to *Love Me Tender*, after a song he sang in it. In other words, he would not become a film actor, he would remain a personality... a sure way to shorten a screen career. By the time Elvis finally tried changing his screen image it was too late."

—Aspiring movie actor turned TV star
Michael Landon

"Elvis was quoted saying he wanted to do *The Jimmy Dean Story* more than anything else and 'I could do it easy.' He was wrong... Elvis wouldn't be convincing as another real person. Elvis was Elvis was Elvis—and stuck with it, for better or for worse."

—Columnist **Radie Harris**

"Elvis had sort of a fixation. He [was]... fascinated by how James Dean died young and became more popular than he'd ever been alive."

—**Natalie Wood**

"Who wouldn't dream of a date with Elvis Presley—how exciting! But when it happened, he had no conversation and I think he would much rather have been alone watching television."

—Co-star **Ursula Andress**

"Let's just say Mr. Presley was rather insecure where women more or less his age were concerned."

—Dancer/actress, co-star
and EP date **Juliet Prowse**

"He was given way too much leeway… a man heavily into drugs, a man who would now be classified as a pedophile for his many assignations and 'dates' with girls who weren't even 16.

Priscilla admitted that after she fell asleep one night waiting for Elvis to finish his karate class, he took her aside and put a bunch of 'white pills' in her hand and told her, 'I want you to take these,' that they'd help her stay awake. But not to tell anyone. Irresponsibly and illegally dispensing drugs to his underaged girlfriend. Some role model."

—Writer **Albert Goldman**

"On nights when we had dates I would be sitting there in my frilly little dresses and girls would come in half undressed… It never really bothered me because the way I was raised these other girls could do things that I wasn't going to do, nor did he ask me to… I wasn't ready for anything like that."

—Underage girlfriend **Sandy Ferra**

"Elvis was highly sexed and used to being catered to… When it came to females he definitely discriminated. He divided them into tramps or into good girls and good women—the good girls were virgins, the good women were mothers… he avoided crossing the fun-time line beyond the tramps."

—Comedian **Nipsey Russell**, who opened for EP in Lake Tahoe

"He'd failed publicly. Failure was new to Elvis, but now he'd gone and failed at the most important thing in American culture: marriage. It had to have been devastating."

—*American Bandstand* host **Dick Clark**

Boze Hadleigh

"Yes, he was [uncircumcised], no doubt about that...
Two others [from his entourage] said he sometimes
worried about his foreskin getting stretched too far.
How, I couldn't say."
—**Steve Dunleavy**, who wrote
Elvis: What Happened? based on information
from insiders Red and Sonny West and Dave Hebler

"Some in his inner circle felt Elvis would have married
sooner, except for the Colonel. He knew that so long as
Elvis was single, female fans from 14 to 40, 50 or 60 could
fantasize, have hope... On the other hand, Elvis was so
promiscuous I doubt he'd have married much before 30."
—**Lil Smith**, *Teen Bag* magazine editor

"Elvis' marriage wasn't meant to, it couldn't last. He
was far from an ideal husband. Or an ideal boyfriend. It
was simply the expected thing for him to finally do, and
it reaped a mountain of publicity and made him more
mainstream... besides, he wanted to be a daddy."
—EP's first leading lady, **Debra Paget**

"Would Elvis have wanted a son? I'd say because of his
relationship with his mother, he much preferred what he
got: a girl. Somehow a boy might have been a threat or
a disappointment to him, without meaning to be. Elvis
had his psychological quirks."
—Psychiatrist **Jerome Motto**

"Six days after the divorce Elvis was admitted into a
Memphis hospital. Semi-comatose. I think the shock of
a broken marriage and that he couldn't hold a wife set
his downfall in motion."
—Singer **Johnnie Ray**

"At the funeral when Elvis' uncle died… there sat Elvis and Priscilla, looking like twins. Elvis had blue eyes, Priscilla had blue eyes. Elvis had his hair dyed coal-black, Priscilla had her hair dyed coal-black."

—**Geraldine Kyle**, close friend of
EP's stepmother Dee Stanley

"Elvis treated Priscilla like a doll… he'd tell her what to wear or he'd have to approve it. But his taste was in his mouth… I remember one outfit of hers that Elvis was pleased as punch about. It was virgin-white but a mini dress with a bare midriff and little pompoms hanging down, and the S&M-type footgear had ankle straps. Godawful! It made her look like a tart—which is the look Elvis favored."

—Psychologist **Betty Berzon**

"You look at their wedding photos and her raccoon eye makeup is so over the top. She had to be embarrassed about it, later on… Later on, when Priscilla developed some independence, she got a much more natural, attractive look to her makeup, hair and clothes."

—**Larry Hagman** of *Dallas*, on which Priscilla Presley appeared

"They married in 1967, were estranged by 1971 or '2, decided to divorce in '72, then divorced in '73. I'm surprised she was able to stick it out that long. Probably because of their daughter."

—Movie producer **Allan Carr**

"Who can say how often Elvis cheated during his marriage? She of course was supposed to look the other way. But when Priscilla fell in love with another man [Mike Stone], Elvis couldn't accept or comprehend it... he was supposed to be the most lovable man on the planet."

—*Spinout* co-star **Deborah Walley**

"*He* filed for divorce. I'm sure that was for his ego and Priscilla agreed. She may have been considerably younger... she was considerably more mature. In a way the divorce was the start of her life—her own life... The divorce, according to most who knew him, was the beginning of the end for Elvis."

—Manager and producer **Sandy Gallin**

"Elvis and Priscilla shared custody of Lisa Marie. But Priscilla and Lisa Marie both left Graceland, and that was... real heartbreak for him... Fortunately he didn't try for sole custody... he couldn't, thanks to the hidden truth about his drugging and sexcapades. Elvis was a doting father and really spoiled his daughter, but his lifestyle and habits came first."

—**Lamar Fike**, member of EP's entourage

"Dr. Nichopoulos found out Elvis was getting near-daily injections of Demerol from some doctor in California that 'Dr. Nick' knew nothing about... Elvis was always determined to get his own way. He liked having his little secrets."

—EP biographer **Steve Dunleavy**

"Later in life Elvis learned how to seem real confident. But he always had some things he didn't like others to know... if you knew them, you weren't ever to refer to them. Like, he didn't like having white hairs, when they came in, and later having white hair... he was a lousy swimmer, didn't like four-syllable words... didn't like it mentioned that he dyed his hair even though everyone knew he did..."

—Stepbrother **Rick Stanley**

"Elvis Presley played a lifeguard in *Fun in Acapulco* and did a couple of movies set in Hawaii... so I was somewhat surprised that he'd never learned how to swim."

—**Angela Lansbury**, EP's mother in *Blue Hawaii*

"Elvis purportedly began using amphetamines in the army in Germany. They didn't require a prescription then and weren't uncommon among soldiers... Elvis didn't have the longest attention span when he wasn't performing, and amphetamines helped keep him awake and attentive for the long periods the army demanded.

But they interfered with his sleep patterns, which were already erratic and troubled. One drug led to another... Besides, amphetamines often produce symptoms of paranoia."

—Music critic **Sharon Tveidt**

"You're displaying some pretty bad judgment."

—**Dr. George Nichopoulos**,
who'd prescribed the 25 or so pills EP
would ingest daily; after "Dr. Nick" took
away his pills Elvis reacted by shooting at him

"The new movie *Elvis and Nixon* [2016] is partly about Presley's supposed 'war on drugs'—that was being waged in his own home! Elvis wanted to feel important and get a shiny new badge from the U.S. president. He also wanted to be an undercover narcotics agent. Undercover—like no one would recognize Elvis Presley, right?"

—Publicist **Andrea Jaffe**

"*Elvis and Nixon* was the first inkling many people had of how far-right Elvis Presley had gone. His shooting at televisions with a gun when the news displeased him was often directed at anti-war peace activists, symbolically killing them... Funny that Elvis was gung-ho for any war a presidential administration declared even though he'd hated every minute of being a soldier."

—**Kevin Spacey**, who portrayed Nixon

"Elvis died in 1977, 40 years ago. I prefer to think he'd have evolved in his thinking... but how much do most people evolve? More likely that he'd have supported any man for president against Hillary Clinton, even *this* one."

—**Susan Sarandon**

"I wonder if Elvis Presley ever voted? An anonymous source from Memphis said he didn't. So who knows? But if he did, I hope he voted for his own candidate, not the Colonel's."

—TV host **Stephen Colbert**

"You can't have a star like that doin' stuff like that, spendin' their time... Once they get to a certain point, they don't have time for none of that... If his fans were dumb enough to believe Elvis sat there and autographed each and every photograph, then I don't have sympathy for anyone so gullible."

—Colonel **Tom Parker**, on Presley's supposed autographs

"Long ago I wanted an autographed photo of Elvis Presley. I was surprised when I was asked, first, to pay for it. I did anyway."

—**John Travolta**

"Elvis got spoiled. He ended up always quitting work at six o'clock. Little or no rehearsal time. Four weeks to make a movie. He stopped caring and stopped listening to his directors. His manager started hiring directors who deferred to Elvis... to the point that one day a movie stalled because Elvis wasn't on-set but the director was too intimidated to tell an assistant to go to Elvis' dressing room and tell him he was needed on the set."

—Actress **Nanette Fabray**, whose niece Shelley Fabares co-starred with EP more than once

"Elvis Presley was widely reported to have been much taken with his *Jailhouse Rock* co-star Judy Tyler, who perished in an automobile accident all too soon after filming wrapped... For whatever reason, Mr. Presley chose to forego her funeral."

—Columnist **Jean Boule**

"Elvis was shocked and saddened by Judy Tyler's death. The only reason he didn't attend her funeral was he didn't want to draw the press and disrupt the proceedings."

—Cousin **Billy Smith**

"I usually play villains. That intrigued Elvis Presley when we did *Love Me Tender*, his first movie. He asked how people reacted to me in real life. I admitted many of them assume I must be a rotten person. Elvis admitted he'd love to play a meanie but he couldn't stand being hated by the public.

I told him he had a guaranteed career in movie musicals. Elvis made a face and said he'd like an acting career, but not in musicals."

—**Neville Brand**

"Elvis [whose mother she played] knew I'd been a star... I felt affectionate toward him. He confided that most of the pictures he'd made had been boring to work on. Ours was a treat or a change of pace because he got to play identical cousins. One had ink-black hair, one was sort of blond... We had fun, and I think the hillbilly theme of *Kissin' Cousins* [1964] appealed to him."

—**Glenda Farrell**

"I didn't see eye to eye with producer Sam Katzman, known as 'king of the quickies.' He had a TV mentality, not a motion picture one. How much better a production we'd have had with a different script and producer and better music. *Kissin' Cousins* took two and a half weeks to shoot, which is nothing to be proud of.
Rock 'n roll was exciting, and Elvis was all about rock 'n roll. But by the time of *Kissin' Cousins* rock 'n roll music was absent from his films."

—Director **Gene Nelson**

"Elvis' movie characters bore what he and Parker called 'real American' names. He might play a Jodie or a Lonnie, which are also girls' names. But his last names were almost invariably Anglo—Rogers, Richards, Carpenter. Non-ethnic... never Italian, Slavic, etc.

Was that a form of bigotry? Nobody even

questioned such choices then. I'd say it did come from bias. If it were done today, and so often, it would be an issue."

—*As Is* playwright **William M. Hoffman**

"Was it hypocrisy or he spoke too soon? Elvis Presley said he wouldn't marry—didn't say he wouldn't date— a girl who wore makeup. Then he marries Priscilla, who wore more makeup than anyone... Eventually she stopped being a Stepford wife."

—Author **Kate Millett**

"For eight years from the time they met in 1959, Elvis kept this girl on sort of a retainer to be his future bride when and if he decided to marry... Priscilla Ann's stepfather, a military man, had moved his family to Germany. She was 14 [EP publicly said 16] when Elvis started with her, and the 1967 marriage lasted about six years."

—Biographer **C. David Heymann**

"Priscilla Beaulieu was the picture of innocence, a 14-year-old in a sailor suit, when Elvis first laid eyes on her. For six months Priscilla and Elvis spent long evenings in his bedroom, talking intimately and smooching passionately."

—*Look* Magazine

"Elvis was so flattering, very convincing. I did think I was the only one. But then I read he did not have one girlfriend at a time—he had two or three, and also one in his home city in the USA... But it did not break my heart."

—German starlet **Vera Tschechowa**, 18

Boze Hadleigh

"Whenever Priscilla's age was brought up, Elvis would say she was real mature for her age. He always called her stepdad 'Captain, sir,' and told him he didn't have to worry. Elvis said he'd take good care of her."

—"Memphis mafia" member **Red West**

"After he was through courting the underaged American in Germany, Elvis returned to the U.S. He handed Priscilla his combat jacket and said, 'It shows you belong to me.' He told her to write letters to him on pink stationery. According to Priscilla, 'Then he disappeared. Just like that.'"

—TV reporter **Ruth Batchelor**

"On his discharge from the service Elvis gave a press conference for 200 reporters at Fort Dix, Texas... They asked about Priscilla, since the relationship hadn't remained a secret. He declared, 'I am fond of Priscilla. But I have no plans to call or write her. I don't just date 16-year-olds.' She was 14. Back in Germany, when Priscilla was informed of that she said, 'I felt suddenly sick.'

Elvis wasn't alone at the press conference. He bantered and flirted with actresses Tina Louise, later of *Gilligan's Island*, and Nancy Sinatra, a future co-star."

—Columnist **Lee Graham**

"His reputation with girls wasn't good... but he behaved like a gentleman with my sister. The guy was afraid of my father."

—**Frank Sinatra Jr.**

"Elvis plunged back into performing a few weeks after his discharge. Ironically his first appearance before an audience was on ex detractor Frank Sinatra's Timexsponsored TV special. The Colonel got him $125,000 for the gig… When Ed Sullivan had finally bowed to ratings pressure and allowed Elvis on his show, the Colonel demanded $50,000—ten times what Sullivan was prepared to pay. That was for three appearances, and as everyone at the time knew, Ed was so upset he didn't appear on his own show the first time that Elvis did.

But this was post-army, and everyone was eager to view the 'new' Elvis. And it was a new Elvis. Not Elvis the teen idol, but an Elvis for their parents."

—Columnist **Shirley Eder**

"For five years, while her man played Hollywood Casanova, Priscilla Beaulieu trained to be Mrs. Elvis. From the time she moved into Graceland at 17, Elvis expected her to be one part servant, one part sex kitten and one-part naïve schoolgirl, oblivious to his womanizing."

—Journalist **Charles Hirshberg**

"When Priscilla turned 15 Elvis asked her stepfather if she could move in with him. The answer was no. She moved in at 17. But what kind of parent or guardian?... It would still be five years before Elvis did the right thing."

—TV host **Art Linkletter**

"Thanks to the freebie-loving Colonel the Aladdin Hotel in Las Vegas hosted the Presley marriage… There's a photo of the newlyweds at a banquet table with a mic and a magic lamp in front of them. Priscilla, wearing more eye makeup than Elizabeth Taylor ever dreamed of, is holding her hand in a strange way, toward her jaw. But not so strange when you realize she's showing off her flashy ring. Her other hand is

Boze Hadleigh

imprisoned between Elvis' two hands, and he of course is doing all the talking."
—Talk show host **Virginia Graham**

"Colonel Parker dominated the day of the marriage… Following the nuptial rites, Parker rushed Elvis and Priscilla to a press conference where Presley (having been coached) answered questions about his personal life. A reception ensued, its guest list comprised mostly of Parker's cronies and business associates. In her autobiography Priscilla wrote, 'I wish I'd had the strength then to say, 'Wait a minute, this is our wedding, fans or no fans. Let us invite whomever we want and have it wherever we want.'

She added, 'It seemed as though as soon as the ceremony began, it was over.'"
—from **Boze Hadleigh's** book *Celebrity Lies!*

"If he was no longer a rock 'n roll rebel, the '60s Elvis was still fairly wild. People expected that marriage would further tame him. But months after his marriage a car was set on fire on the grounds of Graceland—probably Elvis and the boys horsing around—but also, Elvis himself beat up a yardman. Time and matrimony didn't kill off Elvis' inner demons."
—Writer **Shana Alexander**

"I felt sorry for Elvis because he didn't enjoy life the way he should. He stayed indoors all the time."
—Fan **Muhammad Ali**

"Elvis was like a prisoner. He couldn't get out and do things like other people. Wherever we'd go, people were there."
—Entourage member **Red West**

108

"In light of how very young many of Elvis Presley's dates were and how many girls and grown women there were, it's just as well he didn't socialize in public... On top of that, he almost never dated a celebrity, so there wouldn't have been as much interest."

—Columnist **Dorothy Manners**

"How much of Elvis' unexpressed anger at Colonel Tom Parker was expressed at others? I still wonder if the Colonel wasn't blackmailing Elvis... and if so, I surmise it had to do with female minors. It's been duly noted that Elvis' ideal age for dates and sex partners was 13 to 16... Parker hushed up plenty of what went on. One way or another he maintained a lifelong stranglehold on Elvis."

—**Emily Sisley**, psychologist and writer

"The law and the media for the most part turned a blind eye toward men with girls under 18 or even 16. Not any more. What Elvis got away with then he could never get away with today."

—**Jim Graham**, attorney-politician

"I don't know about other men—pedophiles—but when I'm asked why Elvis preferred girls, I'm inclined to say because for him, women were mamas."

—**Dr. Betty Berzon**

"Priscilla knew about Elvis. But the 'reward' of snagging the #1 bachelor must have been worth it to her. She reportedly didn't worry about his quickie affairs and was only bothered by his relationship with Ann-Margret.

I doubt if even that was a major anxiety. Priscilla

Boze Hadleigh

knew Elvis wouldn't marry an actress and why would or should Ann-Margret give up stardom?"

—Carrie Fisher

"Elvis' attitude toward marriage parallels a ridiculous quote given by an overpaid basketball player who said, 'My wife is married, I'm not.'"

—Journalist **Lance Loud**

"You want ridiculous? Watch Presley in 'his first period picture,' as it was called. *Harum Scarum* [1965]. He's some sort of reincarnation of Rudolph Valentino, in a sheik get-up, running around the desert wearing as much eye makeup as his leading ladies... Elvis is visiting some Arab kingdom where he romances the dictator's daughter, prevents a political assassination and sings umpteen songs that you'll never hear again—with any luck.

They filmed this in 18 days. I'm surprised it took that long, except maybe for getting into the costumes."

—Film writer **Paul Rosenfield**

"Even compared to some previous Presley turkeys, this one almost sheds feathers from the start."

—The *New York Times* on
Frankie and Johnny (1966)

"Classy [1969] film title: *The Trouble with Girls (and How to Get into It)*. He doesn't even appear till almost halfway through it. To save himself the embarrassment? In view of his *oeuvre*, I doubt that anything embarrassed him... To call this one a turkey is an insult to our fine feathered friends."

—*Tiger Beat* editor **Ralph Benner**

110

"Elvis did all these made-in-Hawaii movies and I remember a photo of him on a surfboard. I was disappointed to learn it was a fake set-up—it only *looked* like Elvis was riding a wave... and supposedly he never learned to swim."
—Olympic gold-medal diver **Greg Louganis**

"They don't need titles. They could be numbered. They would still sell. That's why he's well paid and gets 50 percent of the profits."
—**MGM executive** who worked on five EP movies

"His first non-musical was *Charro*, a pseudo-western with Presley as a former gang member who gets framed and wears the same costume throughout the film. He's also, for the first time, seen unshaved. It was a change of pace for him, but too late and still not good enough."
—Actor and EP fan **Joel Crothers**

"In one of his last movies Elvis Presley played a doctor. That's so believable. *Change of Habit*—clever title. Mary Tyler Moore played a nun. The plot was will she or won't she give up the habit for Dr. Elvis? Thank goodness in 1969 he gave up the habit of bad moviemaking."
—Comedian **Bob Smith**

"Desperation was proved by the fact that between September, 1969, and January, 1970, three more Elvis Presley movies were released. To shrinking audiences, mostly women who'd been teenagers in the 1950s. Younger people thought Elvis was a square, like his movies... Those were his last three movies."
—Singer **Glenn Hughes** of The Village People

"My wife dragged me to a couple of his movies. I told her if she did it again I'd start calling him Elvis Putzley."
—Comedian **Don Rickles**

"On Elvis' 30th birthday in 1965 the number-one song in the U.S. was the Beatles' 'I Feel Fine.' It was their fifth #1 song in a row. They broke his record. It must have been rather a depressing birthday for him... Later that year the Fab Four visited Elvis at his Bel-Air home and the five of them had an impromptu jam session that everyone seemed to enjoy. But by then Elvis, at only 30, mind you, was a virtual relic of 1950s rock 'n roll."
—British singer **Dusty Springfield**

"Poor fellow. His 30th and 40th birthdays were awful for him, particularly the 40th—into middle age... At least he was spared a 50th."
—Songwriter **Hugh Martin**

"It's not hugely publicized that months after turning, 40 Elvis had a face lift. It might have been better known had the result been more obvious... Fat ages a person. For a face lift to yield maximum effect one can't have a fat or chubby face."
—**Jackie Collins**

"Of course Elvis was jealous of the Beatles. But not just their success. They wrote their own songs... That talent level was beyond him, and he knew it. He didn't hold it against them, but he did resent their being foreigners who outsold him in the USA."
—**Michael Houser**, guitarist and founder of Widespread Panic

"He did not hate the Beatles. But he didn't like them as competition… The one he criticized the most—not publicly, of course—was John Lennon, the most talented one."

—Jazz pianist **Oscar Peterson**

"When Elvis Presley became famous his sideburns were considered extreme and his hair was too long for many of the critics. In the next decade the Beatles had the haircuts that so many American critics said were for girls, and Elvis made some on-the-set comments agreeing with them. I thought that was immature and hypocritical."

—**Fabrizio Mioni**, EP co-star in *Girl Happy* (1965)

"Elvis was an opportunist. You have to be, to succeed. When they turn left, you turn left. When they turn right, you go right. Singers do it a lot of the time. Most actors do it all of the time. With good actors it's something the public seldom perceives."

—**David Bowie**

"Some outsiders like to put down the so-called Memphis Mafia. But it wasn't us was the bad influence…. Nobody turned anyone else onto drugs. But if Elvis wanted drugs he knew how to get them and it all started out legitimate, with doctors and everything.

Nobody corrupted Elvis. His fame and what he and the Colonel did about it, that's what started the bad stuff… Remember, Elvis started out as our friend. Course, he was also our employer."

—Entourage member **Red West**

"Sad to say, without medication Elvis wasn't as good, onstage or off, as when he had it. There were times when he was more lucid with the drugs than without them. He was an addict."

—Friend and hairdresser **Larry Geller**

"I'm not sure Elvis had an actual secretary. Reading or writing correspondence wasn't his thing. It was Colonel Parker who had secretaries, male secretaries. Elvis had nothing to do with those guys, and that suited Parker. But professionally, Elvis didn't want to deal with women except, necessarily, as leading ladies."

—**A former secretary** to Goldie Hawn

"Elvis trusted his boys and relied heavily on them. However, an element of paranoia gradually crept in. The thing he hated most was betrayal. Or its possibility."

—Co-star and friendly acquaintance **Bill Bixby**

"Stars can't become publicly enraged, so some of them take it out on their paid minions. Ask people who've worked as stars' assistants, companions, secretaries, household staff, etc. The stories they could tell! Except for the confidentiality agreements they're forced to sign when they're hired... Regarding Elvis Presley, he considered obedience loyalty."

—Writer **Sheridan Morley**

"Elvis didn't like hiring new people. Could he trust someone new? Did they look down on him? What was their motive in working for him? Did they have his same values and outlook? Besides, they didn't know him through his ups and downs, probably couldn't relate to his moods. And: they might *tell*."

—Studio executive turned producer
Allison Shearmur

"Elvis endured because he came back big as ever. To do that, you have to have a period when you're out of favor. Elvis was up during the '50s, then down with those movies in the '60s, then up again in the '70s, then higher up after he died. It was a classically successful career trajectory."

—Writer/director **Nora Ephron**

"I didn't like him at first. I thought he was vulgar… doing it on purpose, for attention. Movement made Elvis Presley so memorable. But so controversial. He moves less now, that comes with time and growing up."

—Comic actress **Martha Raye**

"The night before he reported for induction into the army Elvis hosted a private blowout at Memphis's Rainbow Rollerdrome. Dividing his friends into two teams, he gave the signal and each side tried to knock the daylights out of the other."

—*Life* Magazine

"One of his songs had a lyric about 'tigers play too rough' and how he preferred a gentle teddy bear. Well, Elvis didn't care for all the teddy bears that fans sent him and he did like to play rough sometimes."

—**Sam Katzman**, one of EP's film producers

"In 1956 at a gas station [a man] slapped Elvis on the back of the head. He had minimal provocation, but then Elvis retaliated by socking the man, an older man, in the eye. It went to court, Elvis was acquitted, and the man had to pay a fine.

Publicly, Elvis stated, 'I'll regret that day as long as I live.' Privately, he gloated… It showed him what he could get away with."

—*People* editor **Richard Stolley**

"One thing that may have saved Presley's life was, after James Dean died Elvis became more cautious at the wheel… eventually he was chauffeured around. Dean was known to be a reckless driver, but after him Elvis didn't enjoy crazy stunts and racing or joyriding as much."

—Car collector **Jay Leno**

"I had Mr. Presley read a scene from *The Rainmaker*. When he finished he informed me that he didn't like the part. The character was too upbeat and 'lovesick.' I asked what sort of character he would rather play? He said somebody more like himself, so he wouldn't have to do any 'excess acting.'

As it transpired, his first screen role was a somber young man who died prematurely."

—Producer **Hal B. Wallis** (Oscar winner
Burt Lancaster starred in *The Rainmaker*)

"My brother was rich and famous before Elvis and he also had a movie career. Neither was an accomplished actor… Rick wrote some of his own songs. Elvis only sang others' songs… Both died tragically young. I think the big contrast between them was dynamism. Rick was so laid-back that it didn't always register. With Elvis, he pushed the 'sex button' from day one. He often pushed the envelope, period."

—**David Nelson**

"There never was a rivalry between me and Elvis, not at any time. That was made up, to sell magazines… One comparison said something I've never forgotten: that the average American girl might fall for either of us but she'd be safer with me than Elvis. When I heard that, I took it as a compliment. Now I'm not so sure."

—Rick Nelson

"Ricky Nelson was a better musician than Elvis. A fact. Who was the better singer, that's an opinion."

—Singer **Rosemary Clooney**

"Stardom seems to excuse anything. It's like Joan Crawford receiving a Mother of the Year award… Elvis Presley through the 1970s was a member in good standing of the International Narcotics Enforcement Officers Association, an American outfit. Yes, Presley was an anti-drugs officer… also a drug addict."

—**Michael Friedman**, artistic director at New York City Center

"I considered inviting Presley to guest on *The Beverly Hillbillies* after hearing he liked the show. But I was persuaded not to try, told he'd be highly offended. Even though he got his start with rockabilly music. Contradictions…."

—TV producer **Paul Henning**

"He may not have started out a prude but Elvis Presley did become rather prudish and very private and fussy about sex. Yet the sexual pre-revolution during the staid 1950s was led by two figures: Elvis Presley and Brigitte Bardot. They expanded what was permissible in terms of sexual suggestion... The more condemnation they received, the more influence they had and the more the general public's boundaries were broadened.

—Author **Ruth Benedict**

"Do you know, even a lot of lesbians found Elvis sexy. Some liked how he presented, and tried to copy his look... Most gay men I've known had a crush on him, whether or not they were into his music."

—Journalist and gay historian **Jim Kepner**

"He is a sex symbol for all seasons."

—**Cary Grant**, who though retired appeared
briefly in the movie documentary
Elvis: That's the Way It Is (1970)

"Oh, I think anyone at all can have a crush on Elvis Presley. Why not? It has nothing to do with his music. Well, not always."

—Talk show host **Merv Griffin**

"Before I came out, I had to keep under wraps what I really felt about Elvis Presley. As someone who wasn't much of an individual and seemed to have no social conscience he didn't rate high in my esteem. But as an entertainer and a singer who brought sex into music and into performance I thought he was fantastic. I didn't put Elvis down, as so many did, but I had to pretend I was indifferent to him, then."

—**Leonard Bernstein**

"I do not know the context of the very foolish statement Elvis Presley made [in 1959, that he would never kiss a

Mexican woman]. He was uneducated about people he didn't grow up with. Perhaps he thought we were another race… in the Southern United States there was still tremendous prejudice. Remember that Mexico abolished slavery [in 1829] long before his country did."

—Mexican actor **Ricardo Montalban**

"The year after his anti-Mexican comment, Elvis Presley was purposely teamed with [Mexican star] Dolores del Rio. However, as his mother… He played a 'half-breed,' from a Caucasian father and a Kiowa Indian mother. He had apologized, and this picture was a token of his sincerity."

—Film historian **Carlos Clarens**
on *Flaming Star* (1960)

"When I worked with Elvis it was almost 10 years after his [comment]. We both played Navajos, what were called 'Indians.' I think Elvis was by partial origin Native American… He was polite… perhaps by then he had learned something about other cultures."

—Mexican actress **Katy Jurado**
(*Stay Away, Joe*, 1968)

"I directed one of the few Presley vehicles that had any merit… After our film's release he got back to me and said he was very proud he got some good reviews on it. But then he turned around and turned his back on quality material—I couldn't figure that boy out."

—**Don Siegel** (*Flaming Star*)

"Elvis used to say he learned as he went along… as opposed to education and college. He liked being alone so he could try and puzzle something out, then ask someone he regarded high about it, then puzzle it out some more."

—Stepbrother **Rick Stanley**

"In 1964 he decided to create the Meditation Garden at Graceland where he… could go to be alone, to meditate or to converse in private."

—Friend and spiritual advisor Larry Geller

"I was surprised to learn Elvis Presley was into meditation. Perhaps he had a deeper aspect than we thought. But then I read that he asked a close friend if meditation was related to medication…"

—Actor **Jack Soo** (*Barney Miller*)

"His name means 'the force of God' in Hebrew, and his middle name Aaron was the name of Moses's brother, a high priest of Israel."

—Psychiatrist and author **David Rosen**

"Elvis thought the Tao was another word for God."

—**Larry Geller** (Taoism is China's oldest religious philosophy)

"It's something I'd heard, not read, so maybe it was unreliable. I was going to ask Elvis about it when we did *Paradise—Hawaiian Style*. But I didn't ask. What I'd heard was he supposedly thought a Caucasian was a gay Chinese."

—Japanese-American actor **James Shigeta**

"Like many people even now, he believed if you were Chinese, Japanese or Korean origin but American you were still foreign. He didn't *get* it… if you were Irish or German origin you were American… I don't think he read much. Or didn't read non-fiction. I once saw him off the set with a comic book."

—**Guy Lee**, who played a character
named "Ping Pong" in *Blue Hawaii* (1961)

"Elvis Presley had to defend himself against rumors of making racist remarks about colored people. I assume if they were only rumors, they were part of one of the early movements to discredit him. But of course, I don't know."

—Singer/actress **Josephine Premice**,
whose parents were Haitian

"That Elvis and his family and white people in the South used the n-word was a part of everyday life. Up to a point. As a public figure and purported role model, Elvis had to dissociate himself from bigotry… After he mixed with a variety of people I do think he became less bigoted. Except politically. In the 1950s he was for [presidential candidate Adlai] Stevenson. But by the '60s he was extremely pro-Vietnam War."

—**Truman Capote**

"In a portion of an unreleased interview Tom Parker expressed his surprise that Marilyn Monroe had converted to Judaism. He said something on the order of 'How can Miss Marilyn be Jewish now? She don't look Jewish.' But neither did born-Jewish actresses Elvis knew, like Tina Louise or Jill St. John."

—*Newsweek* senior editor **Sarah Petit**

"Odd that Elvis Presley's 'Colonel' came out of the

Netherlands, one of the most socially progressive countries, certainly more so than the States. I suppose even Holland had its version of 'white trash.'"

—UK actor **Alec McCowen**

"Elvis admired Tom Jones because he reminded him of himself. The 'threat' and sex appeal, the lusty women fans, etc. They became sort of friends, or as much of a friend as Elvis cared to have… When they met, Elvis wondered if Tom had had some of the same black musical influences he had? Elvis knew nothing of geography—he asked Tom if there were 'Afro-Americans' in Wales? Tom said the only black man he'd seen while growing up was his father returning home from the mine."

—Singer **Mel Tormé**

"Elvis used to like to make a statement… everybody had to shut up. 'I wanna say something.' Then to the silent and attentive audience he declared, 'Tom Jones is not only a great singer, he's a great man.'

At this point, Lamar Fike, a rotund guy who had been with Elvis for years, said, 'Why don't you two just get married then?'

There were a few intakes of breath, because coming out with a smart remark on the tail of one of Elvis' proclamations wasn't done—especially by the staff. Lamar apologized. I didn't mind. I thought it was funny. The atmosphere recovered."

—**Tom Jones** on visiting EP's rented Hawaiian beach house

"Elvis told a member of his circle he didn't like that Tom Jones had a powerful voice. He meant more powerful than his own. I think that's what kept them friendly rivals rather than friends, because they had much in common, including a poverty background."

—**Ifor Jenkins**, Richard Burton's brother

"Elvis didn't like hearing about someone else setting a record... like with the Beatles... Tom Jones told Elvis about going to a Sinatra concert and not expecting to be acknowledged. But Frank did... 'Ladies and gentlemen, the top-rated singer in the world.' Then he added, 'Right now.' Elvis got a kick out of that. A kind of grim kick."

—EP's road manager **Joe Esposito**

"One of the career things [that] irked Elvis before he went in the army in '58 was he couldn't do what Johnnie Ray did back in 1951. That was the first time in *Billboard* history both sides of a single disk held the #1 and #2 chart spots [via Ray's singles "Cry" and "Little White Cloud"]. Back in 1956 or so Elvis thought he'd be able to do the same thing. But he didn't."

—Key entourage member **Red West**

"Elvis Presley's voice was, as it were, kept in Tom Parker's little gold box and only allowed out for money. As if Parker thought overuse or over-exposure would tarnish it."

—Casting director **Ann Brebner**

"Parker didn't know from charity. He kept Elvis' charity performances to a minimum. He thought keeping Elvis 'exclusive' made him a more valuable commodity. It merely tarnished his reputation."

—Philanthropist **Sybil Brand**

Boze Hadleigh

"Sure, Elvis gave away a car here, a car there, etc., and got publicity for it. I guess he was sincere about it. But there should have been bigger, grander gestures. There might have been, except for his miser manager.

Apparently it made Parker's day when he got free sandwiches out of a hotel kitchen or was able to tip a waiter with a fake-autograph Elvis photo."

—Photographer **Ruth Mountaingrove**

"Elvis would bounce back between being incredibly insecure and amazingly confident. And between being selfish and magnanimous."

—**Marty Lacker**, part of EP's entourage

"Elvis was gifting a couple with his-and-her cars while a longtime employee who'd drunk too much complained that he hadn't been gifted with a car. Elvis didn't like being interrupted; he stopped when he heard the complaint. Suddenly he lashed out and hit the man in the face, leaving him bloodied and crying.

Elvis was shocked at what he'd done. But he still couldn't apologize. He sent an underling to see how the man was doing the next day."

—EP biographer **Steve Dunleavy**

"More famous, more abusive. In the 1970s, during a rehearsal feedback problem, Presley threatened a soundman with removing a kidney if he didn't turn off the sound immediately… The '70s were his downfall decade.

Everyone's heard how he'd shoot at TV sets when he got angry. But he'd also shoot out a bedroom window. Angry, drug-addled, shooting off his gun in the house…"

—Radio host **Connie Norman**

"Elvis came to believe the Beatles were responsible for the hippie movement, which he loathed… He criticized 'suggestive' songs and said the Smothers Brothers, Jane Fonda and their 'ilk' were 'poisoning' young minds with anti-U.S. statements. In fact their statements were anti-war and anti-Nixon.

Like so many less educated people, he bought into the right-wing-ism of Nixon—soon to be impeached—and J. Edgar Hoover, whom he much admired… Back in the 1950s it was Elvis who was accused of poisoning young people's minds and exploiting sex."
                    —Talk show host **Phil Donahue**

"It wasn't just nostalgia, he deliberately cocooned himself down in Memphis, away from New York and Los Angeles… from Jews, different colors and nationalities, women who weren't just sex objects… The older Elvis got, the more intolerant and self-righteous… a sad pattern."
                                —**Joan Rivers**

"He took up karate in the army, in Germany. But Elvis didn't see it, as in East Asia where it's from, as a disciplined form of self-defense with a basis in philosophy. He saw it as both defensive and offensive."
            —**David Ogden Stiers** (*M*A*S*H*)

"Elvis would sometimes attend other singers' shows and enjoy them. Naturally, the performer would announce that Elvis was in the audience and sometimes offer him the mic—'Elvis, come up and join me.' For a duet. The audience would roar with enthusiasm… but no way. Not gratis. Elvis had learned in the army: no free shows. He wouldn't disobey the Colonel's orders."
                        —Singer **Dick Haymes**

Boze Hadleigh

"Twice that I know of Colonel Parker went purple with apoplexy. When Elvis agreed to do a bunch of charity concerts—no fee! And after Elvis was dead and his daughter married Michael Jackson. He kept repeating that Elvis would turn over in his grave and what was the world coming to."
—Songwriter **Ric Marlowe**

"It's the most ridiculous thing I've ever known. Whenever I hear anything about that wedding I shut my ears because it upsets me so much. My boy would turn in his grave at the very thought of what Lisa Marie has gone and done. He'd be hurtin' bad."
—**Tom Parker**, 85

"The P.R. aspect of Michael Jackson marrying Elvis Presley's daughter somehow escaped wily old Tom Parker. He didn't perceive it as a brilliant distraction from Jackson's legal troubles with underaged boys and a way to try and acquire some of Elvis' glory. All Parker saw, with his miscegenationist tunnel-vision, was black and white."
—**Fred Weintraub**, owner of New York's Bitter End nightclub

"I think Elvis would have been disappointed by his daughter marrying and remarrying and so on… and the one to Jackson, forget it. Elvis learned to be live-and-let-live, but her marrying a boy who at any rate was originally black, that wouldn't have set right with him. Elvis would have seen right through Jackson using her for his own ends.

And it would have killed his parents."
—**Charles Bronson**

"During the marriage to Michael Jackson, Lisa Marie spent more time with her ex-husband Danny Keough than with Michael... Why she still claims it was a regular marriage may have to do with loyalty or pity. Or not wishing people to think she was a pretend bride."

—UK journalist **Ken Ferguson**

"At 9 a.m. sharp the Colonel's orderly will report for duty. He's always some immaculately dressed young robot who is loaned to the Colonel by the hotel as a go-fer. One of the world's greatest freeloaders, the Colonel is not content just with meals, rooms, offices, transportation and lavish gifts, he's also very keen on getting his pounds of flesh. For years a whole succession of attractive young men from RCA, MGM and the William Morris Agency have toiled as the Colonel's lackeys."

—EP biographer **Albert Goldman**

"About the Colonel's private life? He didn't have one. He did have the required wife... homely, whiny, overfed—and kept her in her place."

—**Sammy Davis Jr.**

"Was Tom Parker gay? Lived in terror of scandal and boy, could he keep a secret. About his nationality, what crime he may have committed back in Holland, about being an illegal alien, his financial misdeeds... My guess is he was gay and celibate. His being so obese and ugly was great camouflage—who'd look at him and think *gay*?"

—**Stuart J. Thompson**, Broadway producer

"If the whispers are true that Andreas van Kuijk created a new identity after he killed a woman and immediately

127

escaped the continent, it's possible he wanted nothing more to do with women… He was a mystery to begin with and a riddle to end with."

—Playwright **Albert Innaurato**

"He was as much of a married man as he was a real colonel, if you get my drift."

—**Red West**

"People are so amazed at Elvis not knowing what his manager was doing to him. I'm here to say that's not unusual. More than once, I was bought and sold without my knowledge… A singer performs. Everything before and after the singing is organized by someone else. Most of us don't care to be that informed, we have enough to worry about… Elvis wasn't a moron. Neither was I. But we got took by greedy liars who fed off us.

At least Elvis stuck with the same leech his whole career. Better the devil you know than one you don't know."

—**Johnnie Ray**

"What originally motivated the Colonel to do merchandising was Johnnie Ray Enterprises, the first company in pop-music history to create and market products capitalizing on a star singer's name and image… Ray's biggest hit was 'Cry,' so there was a Cry-Kerchief that sold like hotcakes—a sheer hankie with Johnnie's screen-printed face in the middle, a border of musical notations, and corners boasting his hit song titles.

Before that, all a fan could buy were eight-by-ten glossy photographs."

—Songwriter **Hugh Martin**

"Parker turned Elvis into a brand name, licensing 78 different products over the years. In 1956 alone, sales of Elvis-related items totaled $22 million."

—EP biographer **John Micklos Jr.**

"Well, he came from carnivals. 'Hurry, hurry, hurry! Step right up, folks! Let's see your dime, your quarter, your buck!' His methods were crude, he was crude, his touch was golden. Of course, he was his own best client."

—EP movie director **Norman Taurog**

"A very few individuals have the dangerous talent to convince. The Colonel did. You look at a photo of him, nothing. Who cares? But you meet him, you talk with him… this man could sell ice to the Eskimos. That's his big talent, and who knows if the Colonel hadn't snatched up Elvis Presley, might he have done something similar for another singer? Very likely."

—Showbiz dealmaker **Jerry Perenchio**

"I think Parker preyed on Elvis' doubts about whether he had anything new to offer once the Beatles and other younger talents came on the scene. He was able to get even more out of Presley after that… It takes a longtime insider to learn somebody else's doubts and insecurities. Elvis' manager knew where to sink his hooks."

—Co-star **Walter Matthau** (*King Creole*)

"Elvis put up with the Colonel way too long. He endured the Colonel's bad taste. But was Elvis' taste any better? So handsome but eventually he stopped caring what he looked like… got fat and became a grotesque parody of himself. Such a waste. Such a waist…"

—Deejay **David Mancuso**

"After he'd been away from live audiences Elvis admitted to several people he was afraid. His second-biggest fear was they wouldn't like him any more. His biggest was that they'd laugh at him. Ridicule, to Elvis, would be a living death."

—Co-star **Gary Crosby** (*Girl Happy*)

"Elvis relished his return to live performing... but he overdid it. Too many performances, too many tours. By the early to mid '70s he was tiring of it... it was performance for performance's sake—and money's. Money he didn't need... Other than his manager, something drove him to keep on... and on. It might have been fear of falling out of demand if he took time off. Or not being able to go back and keep up the pace."

—Singer **Helen Reddy**

"His late-stage career is a good and sad illustration of the old saying that success is getting what you want and happiness is wanting what you get."

—Singer **George Michael**

"Elvis had a long memory where slights were concerned. He was afraid to bad-mouth anyone in public but still hated Frank Sinatra after he called him all those names when young Elvis became a rival... He did Sinatra's TV special for the money and a big-time intro to the mainstream. But the sting of Sinatra's jealousy and very public condemnation never left Elvis and playing a Sinatra record was taboo anywhere that Elvis might hear it."

—Designer **Mr. Blackwell**

"During the '60s Elvis had a mansion in Bel-Air [Los Angeles]. Perfect for big-time entertaining. My mother used to say Elvis didn't want to improve himself socially. When he got invited to A-level Hollywood parties or even B-level he wouldn't go. He preferred rowdy company or sexual company. And maybe he felt he wasn't good enough."

—Actor **Miguel Ferrer**, son of singer
Rosemary Clooney

"The same year he got married Elvis bought a ranch in Mississippi where he and his paid buddies could dude up like cowboys and ride around and make noise. But in less'n a year he got tired of the place. I'm not sure if he sold it."

—**Slim Whitman**

"I don't think Elvis had an attention-deficit problem. But there wasn't a whole lot going on mentally outside his day-to-day happenings. His impact was large but his personal world was quite small… limited."

—Co-star **Hope Lange**

"He was a grown-up, sexy, sexualized, big money-making boy. He didn't mature that much. His lifestyle illustrated that."

—**Debra Paget**, EP's first leading lady

"When Elvis and a regular girlfriend quarreled or she didn't do what he asked, he'd often up and take a vacation with a different, temporary girlfriend. To teach the regular one a lesson—that no female was irreplaceable. 'Cepting of course his mother."

—Blues singer **Charles Brown**

"Burt [Reynolds] tried to model himself on Elvis Presley. He thought if he could be a non-musical but equally sexy version he could make it in movies and leave television behind… Burt had a violent temper, and I had the bruises to prove it. I remember wondering one time, after a painful altercation, whether Elvis Presley were like that, and if all men were."

—British actress **Judy Carne**,
first wife of Burt Reynolds

"Fame and fortune can make you impatient. You get used to having your way—right away… Elvis paid a couple of his uncles to man the gates at Graceland. One time, they weren't at the gates when he wanted in. He became furious at having to wait a few minutes… and still they didn't come. So he ordered his limo to be backed up across the road and simply driven *through* the gates."

—United Artists music executive **Marilyn Petrone**

"The story about Elvis ordering his car to be driven through the Graceland gates may or may not be apocryphal. I'm pretty sure if he did have it driven through the gates, it was by a paid employee and Elvis got out of the vehicle first. Until his final years he had a strong sense of self-preservation."

—Singer **David Cassidy**

"I remember being shocked when it started coming out that Elvis Presley wasn't always the well-mannered Southern boy he seemed. Some of his behavior smacked of impotence or mental immaturity. Even though he seemed to have everything. A good lesson about the hollowness of gross materialism."

—Poet and songwriter **Rod McKuen**

"Eventually he has to have realized how the drugs and maybe the weight were diminishing his concertizing. And maybe he didn't have the same passion for it anymore... though I know he didn't like to disappoint an audience. But he was getting more and more dazed."

—Songwriter **Johnny Mandel**

"In April 1977 Elvis was admitted to the hospital in Memphis with, among other things, a strained back, milk anemia, gastroenteritis and possible cancer. You have to wonder if he knew the end was near."

—Actress and acting coach **Nina Foch**

"I was in shock. Because before, he would never, ever let on to the audience what his emotions were... He never let it out in public."

—**Priscilla Presley**, after an early-'70s concert in which EP reacted to reports that he was "strung out" on drugs with, "If I find or hear an individual that has said that about me, I'm going to break their goddamn neck, you son of a bitch! That is dangerous. I will pull your goddamn tongue out by the roots!"

"What disappointed me was a 1975 concert in Florida that I flew down to from New York, where Elvis virtually never performed. He did almost as much talking as singing. I was shocked, not just because he rambled and repeated... you go to *see* Elvis and to hear him *sing*. Later it was confirmed that he was doing that more and more. To me it's a cop-out."

—EP fan **Andy Velez**

Boze Hadleigh

"There are many unexplained things about Elvis Presley. We can conjecture, but most will remain unexplained."

—**Bonnie Tiegel**, senior producer
of *Entertainment Tonight*

"I went into the big walk-in shower [after a Caesar's Palace performance]… Through the rush of the water I heard Elvis singing. I thought, I'm going nuts, I've been in Vegas too long—I'm hearing Elvis Presley in the shower… I rinsed out the shampoo, opened my eyes and there he was. He had opened the shower door and was standing there, singing… I was looking at him and thinking, if I tell this story, who's going to believe it?

"Maybe he was checking me out—I don't know. But I closed the door and finished in the shower and then I stepped out to towel down in the main part of the bathroom, only to find that Elvis was still there."

—**Tom Jones**

"Elvis had a lot of curiosity. Not about history or art or stuff like that. But anything to do with music… and other singers."

—**Lamar Fike**, member of EP's entourage

"In his bedroom Elvis would sometimes walk around on his bed, sometimes jumping a little like a kid. He'd do that, with an audience—he loved having an audience—when he was upset about something and sort of ranting and raving over it. Or when he was sharing some juicy piece of gossip or telling a joke or talking about something he found really funny. He gave a good performance."

—Cousin **Billy Smith**

"Newspapers in May 1977 dropped the bombshell that Colonel Parker intended to sell Elvis' contract to pay his gambling debts. In June he proclaimed an upcoming CBS concert special, to be shot during Elvis' next concert tour... Almost right up to Elvis' death he was trying to make news and make deals and make more money."

—Talent agent **Ann Dollard**

"In February 1976 Presley and his retinue flew on his private jet from Memphis to Denver to dine on Fool's Gold Loaves, sandwiches made by the Colorado Gold Mine Company restaurant. They consisted of loaves of bread hollowed out, spread thickly with peanut butter and blueberry jelly and filled with a pound of crisp fried bacon. Presley and co. ordered 22 of them... They didn't even get off the plane for a little exercise: the order was delivered to them on the tarmac at Denver Airport.

The cost of this excursion: $16,000. A year and a half later Presley was dead."

—**Jon Krampner** in his peanut butter
history *Creamy and Crunchy*

"On May 29, 1977, Elvis walked off the stage in Baltimore. Next day a psychic in Boston predicted his upcoming death. In June another psychic predicted Elvis would soon die. These gals weren't necessarily psychic—is anyone? They simply saw the undeniable result of what he'd long been doing to himself."

—Columnist **Boyd McDonald**

"Elton [John] went to an Elvis concert and said he looked like a corpse... and Elvis' orchestra leader told friends after another Elvis concert that 'all he can do now is die.'"

—**Allan Carr**, Ann-Margret's manager

"It's sad how his voice declined… you can hear it on records… from about 1969 to, say, 1973 or '4. The vocal quality… it had thickened, it sometimes trembled, there were notes he could no longer reach, he'd sing a challenging song—when he did so—but take the easier way through it. It was part of the overall diminution."

—Songwriter **Sammy Cahn**

"He was spinning himself out of control… Firing those three guys, and the chickenshit way it was done, was a colossal mistake, professionally and emotionally. Even if Elvis hadn't let his father fire them, a book revealing the truth of what was happening to Elvis was sooner or later inevitable.

Sure, he was hurt by the book, including its facts. But they were hurt by what he let be done to them."

—**Linda Wohl**, Paramount music legal executive

"The Colonel was out for himself, big-time. Vernon Presley was too, but on a far smaller scale. Elvis wasn't going to raise hell if his father skimmed a little off the top… Elvis relied far too much on those two father figures. Neither served him well, though in the beginning the Colonel did help boost him up the ladder more quickly."

—Broadway composer **Jerry Herman**

"Things came to a head when Elvis' cheapskate father cancelled pre-paid airplane tickets for Sonny West's wife and little son. Sonny complained to Elvis, who said he would take care of things, so go ahead and fly, all three, to Texas. But Elvis was furious… not long after, Sonny and Red, Sonny's cousin who'd physically defended Elvis in high school, were fired. Through Vernon.

So was karate instructor and security expert Dave Hebler... Elvis didn't care to get involved, so he and his girlfriend flew to California for a vacation, unavailable to the three men. The West boys were flabbergasted that after so many years Elvis didn't have the guts to tell them himself."

—*Japan Times* contributor **Cliff Harrington**

"That was Elvis' way. He never wanted to be the bad guy. So we just fled."

—**Linda Thompson**,
EP's girlfriend from 1972-'76

"Red tried to curb Elvis' drug use, tried to get him to see reason. Elvis resisted that, he came to resent it. He was in total denial about his addiction."

—Entourage member **Marty Lacker**

"You can't be with a man since childhood and not feel something for him... I just wish he would get well."

—**Red West**

"Elvis couldn't believe the Wests, or anyone, would do an exposé book about him... He felt so betrayed. Never mind what he did, what mattered was when someone did something to him... He went back and forth between rage and shame—the public was gonna learn what he did off stage. It so rattled him that he canceled his next recording session."

—Singer/songwriter **Conway Twitty**

"Was it a coincidence, Elvis Presley dying the day after *Elvis: What Happened?* was published?"

—Actor **Christopher Pennock**

"Their book sold three million copies. For two decades the Wests avoided the media; they'd told their story in print and didn't wish to keep emphasizing it."

—Columnist **Richard Gully**

"You can feel sad for Elvis in that the day before his death the tell-all book came out plus he had to go to the dentist—to fill two cavities."

—**Irish McCalla** (*Sheena, Queen of the Jungle*), briefly friends with EP in the 1950s

PART FOUR:
FOREVER ELVIS

Forever Elvis

More than a few people believe Elvis might have lived longer had he co-starred in the 1976 *A Star Is Born* with singer-actor-producer Barbra Streisand. He was intrigued by her offer, made in Las Vegas, but it's uncertain whether he declined or the Colonel sabotaged the deal by making excessive music-royalty demands. The hit movie would have resurrected Presley's dead acting career and possibly yielded an Oscar nomination. He'd have become less dependent on physically and emotionally grueling live-performance tours increaseingly fueled by drugs and binge eating.

There was the lesser danger of Elvis becoming a parody of himself via his over-the-top show costumes, on-stage karate moves and penchant for police badges and concealed firearms. Even before his death at 42 there were scores of Elvis impersonators. (His father died two years later and the Colonel two decades later.) Post-Elvis, the entertainers became known as tribute artists, and there are dozens of thousands around the world. Within hours of Elvis' death, Vern signed a new contract with his late son's not overly bereaved manager. Tom Parker, who became a serious gambling addict, earned an estimated $100 million handling Elvis but left an estate of about $1 million.

Elvis had four grandchildren he didn't live to see. His only grandson killed himself in 2020, terminating the Presley name. But as an entertainer Elvis lives on. His estate earns more posthumously than he did living. He remains the top-selling recording artist ever and Graceland is one of the most celebrated tourist attractions in the country. As with Marilyn Monroe, premature death resulted in ongoing adulation and new generations of fans, which wouldn't be the case were Presley still alive in his late 80s. Why have there been so many Elvis "sightings" and avowals that "Elvis lives!" and why such a multiplicity of Elvis tribute artists? Because people are reluctant to let him go. The "king" represents more than music, he symbolizes an era when youth found its voice and outmoded Victorian standards and restrictions began to crumble. As a young man Elvis was an innovator, part of a changing culture that he helped to change. The movies pasteurized him but eventually he returned to his performing roots. In charismatic person he reclaimed widespread popularity and interest before death elevated him to a mythic plane few entertainers have ever achieved.

"Eleven days after his interment there was an attempt to steal Elvis Presley's corpse, as happened in Switzerland with Charlie Chaplin. This effort, in a Memphis cemetery, next to the grave of Presley's mother, was dumb and amateurish... Months later, Elvis and Gladys Presley were reburied in the Meditation Garden at Graceland."

—Radio host **Connie Norman**

"Evidently there are courts and there are courts. The charges against the three stooges, or men, who tried to steal Elvis' body were dropped. The court decided they were only trying to prove Elvis' coffin was empty and he was still alive."

—**Beatrice Arthur**

"What is all this 'Elvis lives' nonsense? He's dead. Does anyone factually believe otherwise? Let him be! Remember what he did. Stop pretending he's still out there somewhere, drugging and overeating. Remember the better stuff."

—Agent **Frank Rio**

"Elvis Presley created a whole lifestyle."

—**David Letterman**

"He changed everything—music, language, clothes... a whole new social revolution."

—**Leonard Bernstein**

"Elvis went beyond music and singing to symbolize youth and sex and rebellion."

—**Kathy Griffin**

Boze Hadleigh

"It may be awful to say, but he died at just the right time. His youth was shot, he'd gone all Vegas-glitzy and he got fat. How much further would he have slid downhill?"
—**Dick Gautier** (Conrad Birdie on Broadway in *Bye Bye Birdie*)

"Elvis Presley's death deprives our country of a part of itself. He was unique, irreplaceable."
—President **Jimmy Carter**

"Elvis dug his own grave."
—**Billy Smith**, EP's closest cousin

"Elvis, like America, started out loving, but later turned on himself."
—Irish singer **Bono**

"It wasn't quite suicide. Elvis Presley committed egocide... Do you know, of all the many dozens of awards he was given, he only showed up once to accept an award—in 1971 from the Jaycees."
—Columnist **James Bacon**

"Die young, and people forgive most of your excesses—or forget them. People remember the singer, they forget the bad-movie actor. They forget the drugs and sex, they think of Graceland and Gladys and the devoted son."
—Cousin **Harold Lloyd**

"When you die young, or relatively young, as Elvis did, it helps your image. Especially physically."
—**Drew Barrymore**

144

"After I met Elvis and described him as a pixie and said he had a little-boy quality I got some flak. I'm sorry, but that was my personal impression... and after he died, I still think of him more as a boy than a middle-aged man... I asked friends not to show me photos of him after he got overweight."

—Natalie Wood

"Shooting Elvis would have been like photographing a woman—he oozed sensuality. He was very masculine, but his face and rosy flesh had a feminine beauty. I never understood why he hid inside those ridiculous costumes. It would have been a wonderful challenge to get beyond the sequins and rediscover the young truck driver who had sparked the sexual revolution on *Ed Sullivan.*

I didn't say all that right then [the late 1960s in Las Vegas]. But if I'd had time to explain my ideas I think Elvis would have welcomed my proposal and... recovered his lost image."

—Gianni Bozzacchi, Elizabeth Taylor's personal photographer

"We didn't become palsy, but our meetings were quite friendly. He was fun to be with. Elvis attended my opening night at the Riviera in Las Vegas. Do you know that his famous $2,500.00 all-gold suit was a takeoff on my gold cutaway jacket? It was his manager's idea—I was never given credit for that.

And Elvis would send me flowers on my opening nights. He really did... I miss him, and he cannot be replaced."

—Liberace

"Poor Elvis was in a rut doing concerts and nothing else. Getting older and heavier, taking fewer and fewer risks—no risks… living off his past glory. People went to see him just to say they'd seen him, like some landmark. He'd probably have kept at it no matter how fat or repetitive, till he literally dropped dead."
> —Co-star **Lizabeth Scott** (*Loving You*)

"A show that consists mostly of a series of postures" [by an entertainer] "too tired or bored to care."
> —Biographer **Peter Guralnick** quoting a review of one of EP's final concerts

"He had dozens of people around him, supposedly looking after him, but he already seemed like a corpse."
> —**Elton John**, who attended an EP concert in Maryland on June 27, 1976

"Elvis Presley did overeat and ignored nutrition and exercise. But, and quite apart from the myriad drugs he ingested, the man had hypertension, high blood sugar and an impacted colon that induced water retention and made it harder for him to diet, if he tried. That had to be pretty discouraging."
> —**Paul Meehl**, clinical psychologist

"[He was] a man suffering from severe depression, someone who… seemed a willing partner in his self-immolation."
> —Girlfriend **Linda Thompson**, around the time of EP's 40th birthday on January 8, 1975

"By his 40s Presley had glaucoma, and in the 1970s that wasn't as contextually casual as today... Fear of losing one's sight was a major cause of depression back in the day. For some it led to suicide."

—Suicidologist **Edwin Schneidman**

"According to his Memphis karate instructor EP was in "perfect shape" for five years until 1975 Elvis starts to gain weight and he don't want to show me he is out of shape. I think he shamed himself. The end of 1975 he goes to the hospital and I lose contact after..."

—**Kang Rhee**

"For whatever reason, Elvis' multiple hospital stays once he was on drugs weren't widely publicized. Sometimes they were reported as due to exhaustion or something minor. In fact, each hospitalization was a steppingstone to his grave."

—Music journalist **Scott Timberg**

"Much of the media was loyal to Elvis. Twice I proposed a realistic story on his lifestyle. Each time, the editor—at two different periodicals— shot it down... I heard a lot of criticism about how he dressed toward the end, those cartoonish outfits and rings on every finger, which looked so ghetto-ish. But I didn't see the criticism in print. Till years after he died."

—Columnist **Lee Graham**

"It is ironic: Elvis Presley's motto was 'taking care of business' but he didn't take care of himself."

—Hong Kong singer **Leslie Cheung**

Boze Hadleigh

"He'd go to great lengths to get pills… This time he dug a hole in his foot… a gaping, oozing hole. I said, 'God Almighty, Elvis, what have you done?' And he said, 'Bet I get some good stuff now.'"
—**Marty Lacker**, member of EP's entourage who sat with him in a doctor's waiting room

"Those last five years… he was just a tormented person… He didn't know how to stop the drugs. And he didn't want to."
—**Lamar Fike**, part of EP's entourage

"People have a choice of remembering the chart-busting, young, and sexy Elvis or the one in the spangled jumpsuits hiding behind the sunglasses."
—**Robin Williams**

"Elvis left behind an amazing musical legacy that spanned genres. Unfortunately, he also left behind several of the worst films ever made in Hollywood."
—Film critic **Gene Siskel**

"I did an interview about the time I was in a movie non-gem titled *Clambake* [1967]. An Elvis Presley flick… I remember thinking and almost saying that this was what I'd sunk to… from a prestige classic like *All About Eve* [1950] to *this*."
—Actor **Gary Merrill**

"Elvis quit movies at the right time… though in reality it could be said that movie audiences quit Elvis. But he didn't know when to stop with the live appearances. He became kitsch. And that gave rise to the whole Elvis impersonators thing. It's a whole industry now, in and out of Las Vegas."

—Betty White

"I would like to do a screenplay based on the so-called life of an Elvis impersonator. But I just can't come up with enough of a plot or some way to make the lead character more than a schlub."

—Screenwriter **Jeffrey Boam**

"I think tackiest of all are the Elvis impersonators who are also licensed ministers and perform marriages in Las Vegas and other gambling centres. In those horrible white outfits with the flared pant legs and the up-thrusting collars."

—Lynn Redgrave

"The impersonators began sprouting like mushrooms even before Elvis' death. That's got to have been at least a little mortifying for him."

—Michael Hutchence, INXS singer

"Elvis Presley's death came as a shock to most people. Few people knew the extent of Elvis' addictions and unhealthy behavior."

—Hawaiian singer **Don Ho**

"She not only insulted the memory of Elvis; she insulted her own family name."

—**Vernon Presley**, about Caroline Kennedy,
who entered Graceland after EP's death,
presumably as a fan, and wrote an article
published by *Rolling Stone*

"After Elvis died the *National Enquirer* sent a reporter to the church where Elvis was lying in state, as it were. The reporter was disguised as a priest, and when Geraldo Rivera asked him for an interview the phony priest scolded Rivera for invading the privacy of the mourning Presleys!"

—**Bonnie Tiegel**, *Entertainment Tonight*
senior producer

"I still get asked about my 'relationship' with Elvis [because] the tabloids had pictures of me hanging out with Paul Newman, Robert Redford and Elvis Presley... They'd paste two photos together. I've never met any of those men."

—**Cher**

"An unexpected phenomenon after the death of Elvis is the Elvis 'sightings.' First one or two, then more and more, a whole rash of them. An urban legend: Elvis lives... For whatever reason, some people don't want to admit or believe he's dead."

—Trumpeter **Al Hirt**

"Elvis didn't die. The body did. We're keeping up the good spirits... I talked to him this morning, and he told me to carry on."

—Colonel **Tom Parker**

"If Elvis had suddenly chosen to retire he'd more or less still have remained in the public eye. The curiosity about him is continuous. But could he have faked his own death? Come on..."

—Songwriter **Sharon Sheeley**

"There was a battle royale between the Colonel and the Presleys over Elvis' estate... Somehow the old man didn't believe his misdeeds would ever come to light. But the investigators and the law disclosed what a greedy, conniving, corrupt old fraud he'd been, and how he served himself, royally and for so long, at Elvis' expense."

—**J. Russell King**, *New York Times* deputy editor

"What Parker did was hold him back as an artist, especially in motion pictures. He used Elvis as a mint, churning out money till he ran Elvis into the ground, soaked all the juice out of him."

—Singer/songwriter **Lesley Gore**

"I think Elvis found in the Colonel the authoritative, money-making, seemingly problem-solving father figure he never had in his own father."

—Author **William F. Dufty**

"Colonel Parker earned an estimated $100 million as Elvis' manager. When he died, there was $1 million left in the Parker estate."

—**Malcolm Forbes**

"Everyone here in Vegas was aware that the Colonel was a gambling addict."

—Croupier **Bert Loving**

"The Colonel was one of the biggest users of Elvis Presley. Another was Michael Jackson, who after he got in trouble about the boys he personally entertained he married Elvis' daughter for a while. Even called himself 'the king of pop' because Elvis was the king of rock."

—Journalist **Lance Loud**

"All signs point to yes on that."
> —**Lisa Marie Presley**, answering
> Oprah Winfrey's question as to
> whether Michael Jackson had used her

"People keep comparing themselves to Elvis to try and move up the ladder of success. The comparison almost always backfires."
> —**Jennifer Lawrence**

"Elvis had his time, but I'm Vanilla Ice and it's my turn now."
> —The singer born **Robert Van Winkle**

"I'm the most disrespected singer since Elvis."
> —Country crooner **Billy Ray Cyrus**
> in 1992, the year his "Achy Breaky Heart"
> crossed over

"*Dukes of Hazzard* TV actor John Schneider aims to become a singing star. He's #14 on the charts with his rendition of Elvis Presley's 'It's Now or Never.' Poor choice, John. Great song—Italian, retooled into English—but a poor performance. Sorry, John, you better stick to telly."
> —Radio critic **Tina Vespucci**

"The surprise musical success of sexy David Cassidy, co-star of the TV sitcom *The Partridge Family*, has him being tagged the new Elvis Presley. He and his guitar are a twosome, and David is hip to the on-stage moves that shuttled Elvis from Memphis to the mainstream."
> —*Teen Bag* editor **Lillian Smith**

"There's always a new James Dean or a new Elvis. The newbie gets a momentary ton of publicity. But not fame. Fame takes time… and usually requires a unique persona, not being a new somebody-else."

—Barbara Walters

"That's just foolish."

—Singer/songwriter **K.D. Lang**, on being called the female Elvis

"I don't think Elvis Presley is vulgar or a threat to anyone's morals. But I don't think he deserves so much attention. What has he done? He sings well enough, he enjoys shocking people. Is that so special? Can he claim a voice like mine? I didn't struggle getting people to listen to me. The voice I was given made them listen as soon as I opened my mouth."

—Operatic singer **Mario Lanza**

"Early on, I did compose some of my own songs. A few became big hits… I admire singers who perform their own material—if the material doesn't get to be repetitive… Elvis didn't have the discipline or maybe the inner resources to do his own songs. But he was a first-rate interpreter of other people's words and music."

—Singer **Johnnie Ray**

"As a lyricist, I feel I must note—no pun—that Elvis Presley took unnecessary and disrespectful liberties with song lyrics. He'd change words when he recorded a song and in actual performance would change words, even whole phrases, as his mood struck him. That is simply unprofessional."

—Sammy Cahn

"Elvis didn't know enough to go his own way, except musically. His fame and his yes-men became his whole world. Ultimately he suffocated inside his very limited cocoon."

—Beatle **George Harrison**

"Elvis was a lost soul. Except in music, I don't think he ever found himself."

—**John Lennon**

"Apparently Brian Epstein [the Beatles' manager] told friends no matter what Elvis said publicly, he hated his four boys... all you had to do was look into his green, green eyes."

—**George Michael**

"Elvis earns more in death than most performers earn alive. But not primarily from music. From his former home in Memphis, Tennessee, and the trinkets and memorabilia sold there. Graceland is now a regular high-priced Elvis Presleyland."

—Dick Clark Productions executive
Marilyn Petrone

"After Elvis died Priscilla Presley thought she'd have to sell Graceland [on behalf of sole heir Lisa Marie], since the upkeep was exorbitant. Luckily, someone suggested opening it to the public. So on May 4, 1982, Priscilla was there to welcome 3,000 'guests' who paid five dollars apiece to inspect the first floor of Elvis Presley's former home."

—**Warren Casey**, co-creator of
the musical *Grease*

"The Presley estate has multiplied into a big and intimidating business that tries to monopolize the image of Elvis Presley and how it's presented. They've sued everyone from performers and bars to souvenir-makers and artists... everyone but authors, because books entail public knowledge and freedom of the press and expression."

—Columnist **Herb Caen**

"It's like any time the posthumous profits get big, the greed of a given superstar's heirs expands proportionately, and they hire a board of directors that goes for the gold and they don't want to spare even little nuggets to anybody else... Did you know Elvis Inc. was able to put a stop to most of those velvet-Elvis paintings that used to be so popular?"

—Business advisor **Rick E. Coffman**

"At Graceland it's a whole other Elvis... an image, an icon, an ideal. They've whitewashed him to the degree that it's not really Elvis. Gone are the flaws, anything that would make the average tourist like him less—and spend less."

—Publicist **Andrea Jaffe**

"The word 'whitewashing' has a derogatory sound, which an employee [at Graceland] actually admitted. I mentioned it and said for better and worse, the real Elvis was more interesting than this 'Saint Elvis.' So this employee, notice I'm not giving away the gender, replied, 'Yes. Some of us prefer to say 'rehabilitation.''"

—Actor **Christopher Pennock**

Boze Hadleigh

"David [Cassidy] was a god to me. But then, when we were in The *Partridge Family* he was 20 and I was 10... He became this gigantic singing sensation and was like Elvis Presley, down to the jumpsuit and the arenas filled with fans. He became an international sex symbol and I was in awe of him... Maybe he wanted to be another Elvis, but it didn't work out."

—**Danny Bonaduce**

"Elvis' 1970s costumes derived from that decade's 'peacock revolution.' Jumpsuits and embroidery and capes and jeweled accessories were 'in.' Since then, it's become a jokey, ridiculed look. Would-be Elvises don't dare attempt it... only Elvis imitators can get away with it."

—Costume designer **Ray Aghayan**

"The government let people vote on which Elvis they wanted on the Elvis postage stamp. The white-jumpsuited Vegas singer or the original '50s Elvis? Few were surprised when the vote went to the original."

—Cinematographer **David Phillips**

"The 1950s was a dismal decade but drugs hadn't yet taken over millions of minds and lives. I'm convinced Elvis Presley's excesses and obsessions were drug-fueled. By the 1970s almost everything about him spelled excess. And a refusal to go back while there was still time."

—**Leonard Bernstein**

"Many or most stars don't wear terribly well... fans prefer remembering them as they were during their golden years. Elvis, for instance, whose prime years were the 1950s. The '70s saw his comeback but were also the build-up to his fatal comedown."

—Country songwriter **Harlan Howard**

"My family said people went to see Elvis live because they remembered the king of rock 'n roll. They also went to be amused by the hokey outfits and see what he looked like. Up till the mid '70s he looked damn good. Then more people went to see him to confirm that he'd really gotten heavy and was often acting like a goofball, with his on-stage karate moves and all."

—Singer **Doreen Waddell**

"I think Elvis Presley is better as a graphic image—a photo, a poster—than a singer. What hit home with his fans was how he looked and how sexy he moved. All of that shows in his photos. You don't really need the music."

—**Andy Warhol**

"If he'd been plain but had the very same voice, Elvis today would be just another singer on a list of former biggies. Let's face it. His face was his fortune."

—**Charles Guggenheim**, Oscar-winning documentary filmmaker

"Elvis' hair beneath the dyeing eventually turned white, as had his father's at an early age. Several months before Elvis died, Larry Geller his hairdresser suggested he let his hair grow and revert to white, which would make his hair healthier and dramatically highlight his show suits. Elvis responded that letting the public see him with long white hair at that time would be too drastic, but that he would 'give it some thought.' "Before he could give it further consideration, Elvis died at 42."

—Author **M. Hirsch Goldberg**

"In the '50s Elvis had some puppy fat. It didn't keep him from being handsome or sexy. And he dressed like a stud. In his motion-picture period he dressed like a male model or a Ken doll and the puppy fat was mostly gone but he was less sexy. Then on his TV comeback, with no puppy fat and a man's face rather than a boyish face, he wore that one black-leather outfit, and it did the trick. That one costume switched things around, it revitalized his whole career."

—Designer **Mr. Blackwell**

"He had some sexual hang-ups… We know about his phobia toward women who gave birth. What I'm curious about is his kink for having sex with girls wearing white panties. All I can imagine is it ties in with latent pedophilia."

—EP's *Loving You* director **Hal Kanter**

"Presley publicly stated that he wanted a big family… When he died he was engaged to Ginger Alden. Had they married, they might have had a child. But I suppose if he wanted a third child it would have to be by a third wife, in view of his aversion to sex with a mother."

—**Gore Vidal**

"In terms of Elvis Presley's mother fixation, if his twin brother had been born, Gladys Presley would no doubt have been less cling-y with Elvis. That implies fewer psychological problems. On the other hand, it's up to a secure, healthy adult to prevent an attitude or disinclination from developing into a phobia or obsession."

—Dr. Joyce Brothers

"James L. Dickerson wrote a book about Colonel Tom Parker that told a lot about Elvis. He said Elvis was 'backward for his age,' that he was held back emotionally. He related better to kids and young girls than to adults… He was ambivalent and sometimes resentful toward grown women. With men, he preferred to associate with men he could somehow obligate. You don't think about any of that when he's singing!"

—Costume designer **John Mollo**

"When the divorce was announced, many people thought Priscilla Presley was crazy… they didn't know the inside story. She went and found a man who was interested in her as a *woman*."

—Co-star **Carolyn Jones** (*King Creole*)

"What Elvis liked, he wanted others to like. He got Priscilla to take some karate classes. Bad move, bud. She fell in love with the instructor. After their affair began, Elvis was beside himself and tried to plan the guy's death, even instructed a member of his 'court' to kill the guy.

Thank goodness his orders were atypically ignored. When you think how much trouble Elvis could have gotten into, all from his own doing… very lucky man. And maybe he was lucky to have lived as long as he did."

—Photographer **Herb Ritts**

Boze Hadleigh

"At Graceland there was the time when a female guest was talking. That distracted her host, who was playing pool. Suddenly Elvis snapped and threw his cue stick at her. It hit one of her breasts and injured her. The breast was slightly but permanently disfigured. Yet she didn't sue.

"One of Presley's retainers, when asked to confirm that the incident happened, said, 'Yeah... Elvis was having a tense day.'"

—Actor/singer **Adam Faith**

"When his girlfriend [Linda Thompson] of five years broke up with Presley in 1976 she said he was self-destructive and she was tired of 'babysitting' him."

—French singer **Juliette Greco**

"He let himself get talked into investing in a chain of racquetball courts by his road manager ["Diamond" Joe Esposito] and his pill-prescribing doctor [George "Dr. Nick" Nichopoulos]. The very next year they sue Elvis when the scheme collapses. Yet Elvis retains both employees until he dies. Can you beat that?"

—Business manager **A. Morgan Maree**

"Elvis developed a mania for guns that was only partly driven by paranoia. To him they symbolized power and masculinity. Possibly that related to his need to dye his hair black. He began a gun collection... He also amassed a collection of anti-drug badges; police departments throughout the country were glad to oblige.

Those badges symbolized his utter denial of his own, much-hated drug habit. Much of the Elvis personality was subconscious, the truth hidden perhaps even from himself."

—Pychotherapist **George Weinberg**

Elvis Forever

"Twenty thousand dollars was spent over three evenings in a Beverly Hills sporting goods shop on guns and ammunition, then more money a week later in a Las Vegas gun shop... There were, said Nancy, the Graceland maid, guns all over the house, with a visitor once sitting on one by accident when it was under a cushion in the sitting room.

Then there was the day Elvis turned a tommy gun on a toilet in his bathroom. 'I never did like that toilet,' he said as, hearing the rattle of explosions, Nancy raced upstairs. She didn't like to ask what the toilet had done to offend him."

—From the book *Being Elvis*

"When more money came in, Elvis would start spending big-time again. He'd buy himself a $10,000 jeweled gold belt, he'd order gold bracelets for his by now 16-member entourage, etc., etc., and his father, whom Elvis had put in charge of managing his private accounts, would get out the ledger and wail, 'He's gonna bankrupt us all!'

Vernon did this periodically, but one time when he told Elvis that he'd been on the phone to the Colonel, who was upset too, Elvis shouted, 'Fuck the Colonel!' which was a first. He slammed out of the house and drove off."

-–Biographer **Bob Thomas**

"The chief motive of Elvis' uninvited visit to the Nixon White House was acquiring yet another narc's badge, from the highest official in the land. To whom he'd written a rambling letter that included his thoughts on 'communist brainwashing techniques.' The *Elvis and*

161

Nixon movie depicted him as perfectly sober, which is contradicted by facts and associates. Nor did it mention that Presley turned down Nixon's request to perform at the White House."

—Film producer **Craig Zadan**

"It was said that the Memphis mafia saw more of Elvis than his daughter did… His ongoing extra-marital sex and drug use were driving Priscilla away. But in 1971 she decided to give their marriage another go. The marriage was a bust sooner than the public realized. Priscilla was growing up and Elvis was growing out of control."

—Columnist **Richard Gully**

"He loved Lisa Marie but he often substituted expensive gifts for time. He didn't have to work that often or be away that often. But he was Elvis Presley first, a father second and a husband last."

—Songwriter **Otis Blackwell**

"He would stuff himself to the gills with cornbread and buttermilk or sausage and biscuits and then, after his weight ballooned, he would starve himself for days. He would prepare for performances by taking inhuman doses of uppers, then unwind with equally outsize doses of downers."

—*Life* Magazine

"In Pontiac, Michigan, in front of over 60,000 fans, fat Elvis busted his seams… It used to be that Elvis would diet and lose 20 pounds or so before a concert or tour… By the final years he didn't care anymore… or was incapable of making a successful effort."

—Talent manager **Brad Grey**

"Heaven help you if you said he was overweight, let alone fat… One time Red [West] barely remembered in time to say 'You eat a lot,' instead."
—Cousin **Billy Smith**

"They were loyal to Elvis and served him a real long time. He shouldn't have fired them."
—Road manager **Joe Esposito** on Red West, Sonny West and Dave Hebler, who after their dismissal wrote the book *Elvis: What Happened?*

"When he mentioned her death, Elvis would often curse the fate of his mother's dying so young, at 46… four years older than he would live to be."
—Director **Norman Taurog**

"Elvis Presley was said to be suffering from glaucoma, hypertension, an enlarged heart, clogged arteries and a twisted colon. He was probably taking Percodan (a narcotic painkiller), Dexedrine (a stimulant), Amytal (a barbiturate), Quaalude (a hypnotic sedative), Dilaudid (another painkiller), Biphetamine (an amphetamine) and the devil only knew what else."
—*Look* Magazine

"Who, back then, could have guessed Elvis Presley and Marilyn Monroe would die young? She in her late 30s, he in his early 40s. The difference is, Marilyn never got fat. There are no ugly photos of her. Elvis did, but those photos are for the most part suppressed, and certainly are by the Elvis estate."
—Singer **Teresa Brewer**

"Yeah, I was nervous about playing Elvis Presley... I did my best, I think it worked. We got praise. The script and the hair, makeup and wardrobe people were all excellent."

—**Kurt Russell**

"It was a dream assignment. What guy hasn't wanted at some point to be Elvis? Who hasn't wanted to sing like him? What actor wouldn't want to get paid to enact Elvis Presley? It's just the critics you have to worry about."

—**David Keith**

"I can identify with Elvis. From the outside it all looked easy... He was emotionally complex, and that's the most interesting type of character to play."

—**Val Kilmer**

"A few people scoffed. 'You're blond. You can't play Elvis.' But. Elvis was blond and they did dye my hair. I was playing a guy, an icon, not a hair color. And you play the man experiencing what he was going through in a life that was an emotional rollercoaster."

—**Don Johnson** of *Elvis and the Beauty Queen*, a 1981 TV movie

"Michael St. Gerard has a head start in playing Elvis with his similar pout and lips. The most distinctive physical feature about Elvis, facially, was his lips. The hair, you can dye any actor's hair black and style it a certain way. But if the facial look isn't there, forget it."

—Makeup artist **Desiree Esteban**

"Jonathan Rhys-Meyers, like most British actors, is better at interiorizing a character, be it fictional or from real life. Nobody looks much like any given superstar... If an audience comes away with better insight into what that famous person was like and felt like, then the actor has done his job. The appearance part is up to professsional cosmeticians."

—UK critic **Tony Corkill**

"Characterizing Elvis is a lot about the sense of movement and casual confidence he had... It's a lighter load to carry if you're not in a film where the whole thing's about Elvis."

—**Dale Midkiff**, who portrayed EP in *Pet Sematary*

"I marvel at any actor playing someone so famous and visual as Elvis Presley. No matter how good a job they do, many fans will criticize if the actor isn't a dead ringer... It's the performance that really matters."

—**Reese Witherspoon**, Oscar winner
as June Carter Cash in *I Walk the Line*

"Whatever else I do, it'll be a memorable thing to me—and I hope to some people—that I played Elvis Presley in *I Walk the Line* [2005]. It's like, how many guys have played Abraham Lincoln? This is a little tougher, 'cause no one's seen movies of Lincoln or heard him talk and obviously not sing."

—**Tyler Hilton**

"Michael Shannon worked from the inside out to deliver Elvis' mixture of insecurity, obsession with collecting those narc badges, jealousy, rage over a war that the

country wasn't winning, a desire to assert his own importance… Michael did a fine job. And he said I did a good job as Nixon, who was even more screwed up!"
—**Kevin Spacey** of *Elvis and Nixon* (2016)

"Even Frank Stallone, the brother of the other one, has enacted Elvis… further proof that they're making way too many movies and TV films about Elvis… The more of these portrayals you see, the more you realize it's like donning a Halloween costume… and not that difficult and probably a lot of fun."
—DJ **David Mancuso**

"In *The Fugitive Kind* [1959] my character was Presley-esque. The persona was subtly suggested [by Tennessee Williams]… Biographical films omit most of a subject's essence and experiences, yet filmgoers often leave the theatre with the risible conviction they now know what that person was like."
—**Marlon Brando**

"As a biographer, I'd love to script a movie about Elvis Presley. His reality was more interesting than any sanitized picture could be. However, the producers would aim their product at his fans, who want to worship, not learn. If they want to learn, they read a book, they don't see a movie."
—**C. David Heymann**

"Before Elvis 'went Vegas,' most people considered him sort of humorless. His Vegas look showed he had a sense of humor if not necessarily taste. It brought him down to a more earthy, winky-wink fun level."
—Las Vegas magician **Doug Henning**

"Oh, Elvis loved his little capes and that whole bat-wing look. He liked to dress up... Having basked in the limelight for so long, he was bored, he wanted something fresh and exciting. Those white Las Vegas costumes with all the rhinestones and beads and rivets, the eagles and sunbursts, the plunging necklines, the sewn-in capes and the detachable capes, he loved it. For the rest of his life it became his signature."

> —**Katherine Murray**, cohost of TV's
> *Arthur Murray's Dance Party*

"He did feel conspicuous at first. He didn't want to be laughed at. But Liberace and Elton John and David Bowie were already accustoming Las Vegas and audiences everywhere to the bolder '70s look. It was good showmanship, and Elvis adapted to it. He was a peacock at heart."

> —**Martha Hyer**, widow of Hal B. Wallis,
> producer of nine EP films

"In 1957 he caused a sensation when he wore that gold-lamé suit by Nudie of Hollywood. The man was known for his western-style costumes and used to design for burlesque dancers... The gold costume was more Liberace than Liberace. It flabbergasted his fans and appalled his detractors. It became the cover of a record album extravagantly titled 'Fifty Million Elvis Fans Can't Be Wrong.' That came from the old saying about how 50 million Frenchmen can't be wrong."

> —Singer **Helen Forrest**

"I don't think Elvis was very comfortable in his gold-lamé suit. After all, it was the strait-jacketed 1950s, not the much more flamboyant 1970s... He only wore it twice, and then he wore only the jacket—I mean he wore it with non-matching pants."

—Co-star **James Gregory** (*Clambake*)

"I'm guessing that gold-all-over outfit styled like a man's suit was his manager's idea. It strikes me as right up Colonel Parker's alley."

—*Roustabout* co-star **Barbara Stanwyck**

"A few facts most non-fans don't know: Elvis didn't like underwear and liked to shave his armpits. He also had a habit, when he used to bother opening them, of tearing up fan letters after he read them. Not in half or in quarters, but tearing them into shreds and leaving them lying around for someone to toss in the waste basket."

—EP memorabilia collector **Scott Larson**

"I was disappointed watching Elvis in Las Vegas wearing a huge belt over a big belly. I grew up watching him on TV, a dreamboat... All those crazy stage outfits couldn't camouflage it or his bloated face. It was a real let-down."

—Former fan club member **Joanie Hannigan**

"During one of his later concerts it was all too clear Elvis was on drugs. He made his entrance giggling—at nothing funny—and he'd forget lines while he was singing. The guy tried to be entertaining and flippant about it all, but the spectator-witnesses knew this was the beginning of the end or very close to the end itself."

—Photographer **Helmut Newton**

"He tarnished his image by going on stage weighing as he did. He should have stayed home till he lost the weight. That, or eat all he wanted but quit the business. It wasn't fair to audiences... Leave us our positive memories."

—Irish tourist **Eileen Carnahan**

"Elvis was more square than rebel, despite the early image... He never rebelled in his life. What gave him that image was being loose enough to incorporate his singing pleasure and sexuality into his musical performances... that shaking, wobbly left knee of his was an obvious symbol of orgasmic sexual tension."

—Grammy-winning producer **Tom Dowd**

"Part of the Elvis style is from the Pentecostal churches he and his parents attended. Where a supposed spirit of possession takes over and emotion bursts forth... When Elvis talks, he sometimes sounds repressed. Not when he sings, brother!"

—Classmate **Leroy Green**

"Way back when, singers of both sexes were expected to stand still when they sang, 'specially the guys. Then along came Johnnie Ray, who couldn't and who's so emotionally connected to his lyrics he became an overnight sensation and a target for the media and moralists. Elvis followed in his bouncy footsteps. He was a big Johnnie Ray fan. I doubt he'd admit it anymore."

—Hawaiian singer **Don Ho**

"People put down the Presley movies but if he'd remained just a singer, new styles and the Beatles and the post-Beatles singers and newer styles would have buried him. He'd mostly be remembered as a major 1950s singer... Johnnie Ray was in one major Fox musical and a small role in one of ours, a non-musical. Period. Not many people remember him, though he was very, very big then."

—Paramount executive **A.C. Lyles**

"Elvis' face is iconic. To me it represents sex and a whole era when a new kind of music was fresh. He's not the best pop singer. He's only the most exciting one."

—**Cher**

"I think nostalgia drives the Elvis craze. Whether you grew up with him in the '50s, '60s or '70s or after he died, he's about a simpler, less complicated time. Not a better time, but a more beckoning time."

—**Adam West**, TV's *Batman*

"Same for Marilyn, same for Elvis. Dying young elevated them to a more rarified level of fame and mystique than if they'd lived and aged. We tend to sanctify those who die young."

—Hollywood studio chief **Dawn Steel**

"At least Elvis was born with his rather ridiculous name and didn't have to apologize for it. Like I've had to do."

—**Troy Donahue**, born Merle Johnson

"Do I like Elvis Presley? Sure. A whole lot... Did I name my son after him? Uh... not really."

—Closeted actor **Anthony Perkins**

"I'm Irish and my original name isn't Elvis. Sometimes Americans say Elvis doesn't go with an Italian name. Well, Elvis is now international and my surname is Irish, not Italian. It's pronounced differently than 'Abbott and Costello'—the stress should be on the last syllable."
—Singer **Elvis Costello**

"Dyeing his hair black made Elvis look more Latin... like Don Juan or Casanova or Valentino. That helped make him more popular in Latin America, also Japan. People there could identify with him more."
—**Juan Garcia Esquivel**, Mexican composer who "invented" space-age cocktail music

"Elvis resisted occasional suggestions that he grow a mustache... There was a time they were considered foreign-looking."
—Columnist **Richard Gully**, ex assistant to Jack Warner

"I knew a friend of Elvis' hairdresser who said he mentioned possibly getting his hair permed. Lots of men were doing it... In the end the Colonel vetoed the idea. He didn't want to tamper with the formula. Experiments were *out*."
—Actress **Carol Lynley** (born Carolyn Lee)

"I don't know if it's true, but I heard Elvis had some kind of a test he used to make sure any hairdresser who touched his head was straight. I wouldn't doubt it. From what I heard, Elvis was mighty uncomfortable when another guy thought he was good-looking. Figure that one out."
—Singer **Del Shannon**

"When he started out, everything including the media, was under male control. What women liked didn't, for the most part, matter... the average female liked Elvis. Quite a bit. It was some of the average guys he made uncomfortable. Maybe they feared being attracted to him. The most deep-closeted ones are often the most homophobic."

—Author/activist **Kate Millett**

"I worked with Elvis on *Paradise—Hawaiian Style*... When I'm asked about working with him I have little to say. He was delivered to the set, performed his lines or song, then retreated to his dressing room. He was segregated from his coworkers. That's not unique in Hollywood but I wish I'd gotten to know him. He was very compelling. When he did notice you and smiled at you, you knew instantly why he was a star."

—**James Shigeta**

"I've stopped being surprised that I almost never am asked about Elvis Presley, for whom I designed very discreet costumes... His pictures were moneymakers. Today they're almost forgotten or they're politely ignored."

—**Edith Head**

"I hardly make mention anymore. Relatives, friends, strangers, they all asked, 'You worked with Elvis Presley, what was he like? What was he *really* like?' Finally I had to say, 'He was on best behavior. What would you expect? He was working, on display.'

I don't know what he was *really* like. I didn't live with him or work with him for years —ask *them*. I hardly worked with him at all, and I wasn't his employee. I was employed, very briefly each time, by the film studios."

—Actor **Guy Lee**

"I based a character in my play on Presley: a sexy wandering minstrel whom women found irresistible. But a man more attached to his guitar than to any female... The movie version [*The Fugitive Kind*] was a mite racy for its time and was not a popular success."

—**Tennessee Williams**

"There's a scene in *The Fugitive Kind* with Brando and Joanne Woodward that strongly implied oral sex. Possibly for the first time in an American film... I'd love to know how Elvis felt about that, if he had any hang-up about it... I suppose if I'd asked him outright, 'What do you think of oral sex?' he might have answered, 'I think there's no harm in talkin' about the subject, ma'am.'"

—Comedian **Totie Fields**

"I began work on a screenplay about a singing sensation whose dream of becoming a movie star comes true, but it does him in professionally. Till he walks out on Tinseltown, downsizes and takes up the guitar again. Starting over again, he becomes a sensation once more. Then guess what happens to me... Elvis Presley dies. I put the screenplay to one side. It's still there."

—**Jeffrey Boam** (*Indiana Jones and the Last Crusade*)

"Not generally known... Elvis wasn't a great guitar player. I think he played the piano better."

—Grammy-winning bandleader **Ray Conniff**

"Dying when he did gave a big boost to Elvis Presley's sluggish record sales. So now we can focus on how he sounded instead of on his weight or apparel. And compared to the Elvis impersonators he doesn't seem too commercially crass. The real deal... Like they say, dying was a brilliant career move."

—**Robin Williams**

"For the tenth anniversary of his death I visited Graceland. I was considering writing a screenplay based on Elvis. I gave it up after being sorely disappointed. [Graceland] sits across the street from a strip mall and it's now in a mostly black neighborhood that hasn't benefited at all from the gold mine that Graceland rakes in every single day... It was all so nakedly commercial. Very off-putting."

—**Howard Delaney**

"Down the street from Graceland you could buy Elvis Trading Cards for half what they charge for the same thing at the Graceland giftshops. Nor is Graceland very happy that they have to compete with unofficial giftshops."

—Travel writer **Jessica Charles**

"Elvis had rather gaudy taste, and in the 1970s he redecorated Graceland or part of it to look like a bordello. His ex wife went through the place after he died and re-redecorated it. The result is it's more reflective of Priscilla than Elvis."

—Songwriter **Jay Livingston**
("Que Sera, Sera")

"The Elvis estate doesn't acknowledge black influence on Elvis' music or performance style... He covered some songs already recorded by artists of color, but being more widely played, the Elvis versions became national hits."

—Singer **Barbara McNair**

"In 1997 EPE [Elvis Presley Enterprises] took a cue from Planet Hollywood and opened Elvis Presley's Memphis, the forerunner of a chain of restaurant-nightclub-giftshops. It's a roaring success... You can eat some of the King's favorite dishes, like meatloaf and pulled pork shoulder while listening to his music and watching him on enormous screens, then shop for Elvis souvenirs and knick-knacks."

—Talk show host **Skip E. Lowe**

"We are creating a place where Elvis, who was a consummate host and entertainer, would have enjoyed entertaining his friends between road tours and filming movies. Guests will experience Elvis' hospitality firsthand in an incredibly fun environment."

—**Priscilla Presley** on Elvis Presley's
Memphis ("firsthand"?)

"I read that Elvis' favorite food was fried peanut butter and banana sandwiches. I love bananas so I tried that—it's really good!"

—**Eddie Munoz** (*Malcolm in the Middle*)

"Elvis Inc.'s insistence that its real interest in Elvis is to improve and guard his image is ludicrous, as even a cursory look at the stuff the company licenses and the litigation it pursues suggests. Are $9.95 Elvis Socks and $49.95 Elvis Bowling Shirts… more tasteful than the Elvis sweatsuits that Elvis Inc. refuses to market?

"EPE's real interests are obviously financial: how else to explain its demands that the Lady Luck Casino in Tunica, Mississippi, remove an image of Elvis from a large wall mural or pay a licensing fee of one million dollars a year? The result: the casino opted to paint out Elvis and replaced him with Frank Sinatra."

—Cultural-studies professor **Erika Doss**

"Would the Colonel have approved? The Richard Nixon Presidential Library in Yorba Linda, California, is cashing in on Elvis in the form of wristwatches featuring a picture of Nixon and Elvis shaking hands. That's six hands, total, for only $45, folks."

—Travel writer **Lisa Atterbury**

"In 1995 two groups of skydiving impersonators, the Flying Elvises and the Flying Elvi, were suing each other in federal court. That is how much he is missed."

—*Life* Magazine

"I am not an impersonator, I am an Elvis interpreter. I refry Elvis and serve him up with salsa and reinterpret such classics as 'You Ain't Nothin' But a Chihuahua.'"

—Gay Mexican-American **El Vez**

"I'm not an Elvis impersonator. That sounds cheap, derivative and old-hat. I am one of a number of Elvis tribute artists… artists who pay tribute… People may laugh, but they love it. You can make a good living at it."

—**James Warren**

"When Elvis died there were 170 Elvis tribute artists at large. By the year 2000 it was calculated that this number had risen to 85,000… There is a popular Chinese Elvis who performs in London."

—Writer and broadcaster **Ted Harrison**

"The Elvis imitators have no choice but to wear the Vegas-style outfits Elvis took to in the '70s. If they tried to 'do' him as he was in the 1950s it wouldn't work—you'd see at once they're not him. The gaudy latter-day costumes provide most of the illusion."

—Stuntwoman **Paula Dell**

"The tribute artists' costumes are laughable today but were less so when Presley wore them in the 1970s. That's when men temporarily dared to wear colorful and ridiculous clothes, from platform heels and bell bottoms to pantsuits and low-cut shirts and jewelry on their chests.

If Elvis had survived into the '80s and beyond he'd likely have altered his look. But because he died in the '70s that's the look that's associated with him and with all the tribute artists. Bad luck!"

—Film and TV director **Leslie H. Martinson**

"Elvis going over the top sartorially on his concert appearances owed a lot to the example of Liberace, who was considered a consummate showman. Without the glitz, the glamour and the gaudy, he was just a pianist. His costumes, candelabras, cars and other stage presentations sold the tickets."

—Singer **Billy Guy** of the Coasters

"One reason Elvis increased the flash quotient in his professional wardrobe was his voice was diminishing... he couldn't reach the same notes and the quality was less youthful, less clear-toned. What he wore helped to compensate and distract."

—Jazz musician **Nat Adderley**

"The latest profitable development in the ongoing Presley saga is Elvis look-alikes who officiate at wedding chapels in Las Vegas and elsewhere. For example, the Las Vegas Graceland Chapel offers a 'Loving You' package for $329. The Elvis clone escorts and gives the bride away and sings three numbers.

Other sites offer a Pink Caddy wedding or an Elvis Blue Hawaii wedding... Graceland itself chimed in with its Chapel in the Woods, in the shadow of Presley's home. That package costs near to $800 but omits a fake Elvis—that would be exploitive. Come again?"

—Comedy writer **Jack Burns**

"To prove there was only one Elvis, none of his descendants has made a mark, musically. His daughter tried... I don't know about the granddaughters... His grandson was going to be a singer but that fizzled. Or he did."

—Musician **André Previn**

"Benjamin Keough told the media in 2009 that he'd signed a major five-record deal with Universal. Universal later denied the deal... He had completed one rehab program but attended three or four times and is said to over-indulge alcohol and other drugs."

—**Bonnie Tiegel**, senior producer, *Entertainment Tonight*

"Elvis has four grandkids, all born long after he died. One is a grandson named Benjamin, from Lisa Marie's marriage [of four] to singer-songwriter Danny Keough. Benjamin is known to suffer from chronic depression… a contributing factor may be pressure to emulate his grandfather."

—EP fan and psychology major **Andrea Robb**

"Facts about his personal life are scarce… He's described as a musician. But Ben's produced next to nothing and has two acting credits, one in a Presley-family project… He doesn't seem to be pursuing anything really. His expression is usually blank or glum and he's getting heavy in the face too early. Elvis didn't really overeat until his final years."

—Music journalist **Scott Timberg** in 2017

Due to patriarchal naming: "There is no grandchild now to carry on his Presley name. It is sad Elvis Presley had *one* grandson."

—**Tomiyoshi Nakagawa**, ex VP of a Japanese "Elvis Alive" club in 2021

"Benjamin Keough, who attempted suicide earlier this year, has died at 27 in Calabasas, California. He shot himself on July 12, 2020… The autopsy discovered cocaine and alcohol in his blood... His body is being sent to Memphis, Tennessee. The upcoming burial at Graceland will be the first there since that of Minnie Mae Presley, Elvis Presley's paternal grandmother (1893-1980)."

—Syndicated news item

"Like Elvis, his grandson died in the bathroom."

—Actor **Andy Dick**

EPILOGUE:
IN HIS OWN WORDS

Epilogue: In His Own Words

"They're makin' fun of me."
> —At a 1954 concert, unaware that the
> audience's hooting was *for* him

"I never expected to be anybody important."

"My looks?... I don't think about them."

"I'm so nervous. I've always been nervous, ever since I was a kid."

"We never had any luxuries but we were never real hungry, you know."

"Coach, I hate to tell you this, but I'm quitting the team. I'm a lover, not a fighter."

"I'm not kiddin' myself. My voice alone is just an ordinary voice. What people come to see is how I use it. If I stand still while I'm singin,' I'm dead, man. I might as well go back to drivin' a truck."
> —**EP** to boxing coach Walt Doxey
> after trying out for the Humes
> High School boxing team

"The Elvis Presley National Anthem."
>   —How EP introduced "Hound Dog,"
>   the song that concluded many
>   of his early concerts

"I don't like to be called Elvis the Pelvis. I mean, it's one of the most childish expressions I've ever heard coming from an adult. Elvis the Pelvis. My pelvis has nothing to do with what I do."

"Girls, I'll see you all backstage."
>   —What he often said to close
>   a show during the mid 1950s

"I've made a study of Marlon Brando... poor Jimmy Dean... and myself, and I know why girls... go for us. We're sullen, we're broodin,' we're something of a menace."

"People will come from miles around to see a freak."

"Meditation is better than any drug I know. I can relax, I can breathe deeper, I'm calmer."

"I would like a chapel so my fans would have a place to meditate."
>   —EP's response to lifelong friend
>   Janelle McComb when she asked what
>   he'd like to have done in his memory

"I've always known and now my folks are assured that you are the best, most wonderful person I could ever hope to work with. Believe me when I say I will stick with you through thick and thin and do everything I can to uphold your faith in me."

> —A thank-you telegram to Colonel Tom Parker
> after he engineered the sale of EP's
> Sun Records contract to RCA

"I am the most miserable young man you have ever seen. I have got more money than I can ever spend. I have thousands of fans out there and I have a lot of people who call themselves my friends, but I am miserable."

> —After returning to Memphis following
> a concert tour in the mid 1950s

"I get lonesome right in the middle of a crowd."

"The fans, the fans—they don't know my pain."

"They know about Elvis the image but not… the inner me."

"A long time ago someone very special [ex girlfriend June Juanico] gave me a book to read. I've read it at least a million times. It's my favorite book. I try to keep a copy with me at all times. It's my unwinder. It helps me relax and forget everything."

> —On *The Prophet* by Kahlil Gibran

"Yeah, I'm a Johnnie Ray fan and I appreciate how back when almost no one in the business would say anything positive for me, he was in there telling the public I was a good singer and he liked my music."

Boze Hadleigh

"I've never written a song in my life. It's all a big hoax."

"I'm strictly for Stevenson. I don't dig the intellectual bit, but I'm telling you, man, he knows the most."
>—On presidential candidate Adlai Stevenson
who ran unsuccessfully in 1952 and 1956
against General Dwight "I Like Ike" Eisenhower

"No, I do not think my music causes juvenile delinquency."

"No, Sir." "No, ma'am." "Well, I believe that one takes the cake."—frequent responses to ridiculous questions asked by the press in the mid 1950s

"He has a right to say what he wants to say… but I think he shouldn't have said it. He's mistaken about this, this is a trend, just the same as he faced when he started years ago."
>—Responding to Frank Sinatra calling him
a "side-burned delinquent" and a "cretinous
goon" and defaming rock 'n roll

"Man, all I did is what came natural. I guess if you have a dirty ole mind, that's exactly what you're gonna see in others."

"My moment of glory is being on that stage and singing and feeling all the love the audience sends to me… It's beyond any mortal high."

"Hair today, gone tomorrow."
>—While being given a traditional
army crew cut in 1958

"It's funny. You're ordered to let them cut your hair off, then they expect you to pay for it… 65 cents' worth."

"Caucasian? It was on my army draft card. I thought it meant circumcised."

"Everything I have is gone… She's all I lived for. She was always my best girl."
                                        —Upon his mother's death

"I was an only child and Mother was always right with me. I could wake her up any hour of the night if I was worried or troubled."

"Wake up, Mama. Wake up, baby, and talk to Elvis."
                                        —At his mother's open casket

"I love you so much. I lived my whole life for you. Oh, God, everything I have is gone."
                                        —Words cried at his mother's funeral

"It was my mother's home."
                                        —Explaining why he would never sell Graceland

"I made my father retire. There isn't much sense in him working, because I can make more in a day than he can make in a year."

"The Colonel is almost like a daddy to me when I'm away from home."

"She's got to be American. One who doesn't smoke or drink, a high school graduate—not a college girl—well-bred, warm-hearted, patient and understanding, doesn't use makeup, healthy and energetic, a real homemaker, a loving and devoted wife and mother willing to raise a real large family."

—On what kind of girl he'd like to marry

"I am fond of Priscilla. But I have no plans to call or write her. I don't just date 16-year-olds."

—At a Fort Dix press conference (Priscilla was 14)

"More than anything I want to be an actor. The kind that stays around for a long time."

"They want me to try an artistic picture. That's fine. Maybe I can pull it off some day. But not now. I've done 11 pictures and they've all made money. A certain type of audience likes me. I entertain them with what I'm doing. I'd be a fool to tamper with that kind of success."

"The only thing worse than watching a bad movie is being in one."

"I cared so much it hurt. Hollywood never got who I was. I don't think anybody was trying to hurt me, but they did."

—EP's reply when asked about his movies, "Did you just not care any more?"

"I haven't been in front of those people in eight years. What am I gonna do if they don't like me? What if they laugh at me?"

—Waiting to tape a musical performance before a live audience in 1968

"I like entertaining people. I really miss it."

"I got tired of singing to the guys I beat up in the motion pictures."
> —To the audience, the night he
> opened in Las Vegas

"I hope this suit don't rip up, baby."
> —A line interpolated into his song
> "Suspicious Minds" during his 1973
> "Aloha from Hawaii" concert,
> referring to his overweight

"You need more singers on stage. That's why I've got the fellas. When I go up at the end they go up with me. I could virtually pull out and the note will still be there. I'm covered."
> —Advice to singers who didn't
> use backup singers

"It's not fair I can't go in a restaurant and not be recognized. Eating out used to be a big treat."

"What do you take to keep sane? What drug do you use?"
> —To fellow Vegas entertainer Tom Jones,
> who didn't use any

"Someone to love, something to look forward to and something to do."
> —From EP's handwritten "Philosophy
> for a Happy Life"

"You know, one of the most important things to learn in life is to be able to cope with not having anything to do."

"My life is over. I'm a dead man."
　　　　　—After reading galleys of the tell-all book
　　　　　Elvis: What Happened? by three longtime
　　　　　friends and employees he abruptly had fired

"I'm self-destructive but there's not a lot I can do about it."
　　　—EP's reply when asked his worst character flaw

"No one can live up to that image and survive."

"I don't want to miss out on heaven due to a technicality."
　　　　　—Responding to the question why he wore
　　　　　both a crucifix and a Star of David

About the Author

Boze Hadleigh is the author of 28 books, most of them Hollywood-themed. The *Los Angeles Times* called him "a pop culture phenomenon." He holds a master's degree in journalism, speaks five languages, has traveled to over 60 countries and won on "Jeopardy!" He was born in a British hospital in the oldest city in the world.

Other Riverdale Avenue Books
You Might Enjoy

Inside the Hollywood Closet:
A Book of Quotes
By Boze Hadleigh

Hollywood Lesbians: From Garbo to Foster
By Boze Hadleigh

Hollywood Gays:
Conversations with Cary Grant, Anthony Perkins,
Liberace, Ceaser Romero and Others
By Boze Hadleigh

Hard Work: The Greta Van Fleet Story
By Marc Shapiro

Lorde: Your Heroine, How This Young Feminist
Broke the Rules and Succeeded

Legally Bieber: Justin Bieber at 18
By Marc Shapiro

Boze Hadleigh

You're Gonna Make It After All:
The Life, Times and Influence of Mary Tyler Moore
By Marc Shapiro

Hey Joe: The Unauthorized Biography of a Rock
Classic
By Marc Shapiro

Deeply Superficial:
Noel Coward, Marlene Dietrich and Me
By Michael Menzies

Also by Boze Hadleigh

Elvis through the Ages
Marilyn Forever
Life's a Pooch
Hollywood Lesbians: From Garbo to Foster
Celebrity Feuds!
Secrets, Scandals & Swansongs
Hollywood Gays
Inside the Hollywood Closet
Holy Cow! Animal Words & Phrases
Marilyn: Lost Images

www.ingramcontent.com/pod-product-compliance
Lightning Source LLC
Chambersburg PA
CBHW070035100426
42740CB00013B/2697